REFLECTIONS ON A LIFE IN EXILE

REFLECTIONS ON A LIFE IN EXILE

by

J.F. RIORDAN

FIRST EDITION

Library of Congress Cataloging-in-Publication Data
Names: Riordan, J. F., author.
Title: Reflections on a life in exile / by J.F. Riordan.
Description: First edition. | New York, NY : Beaufort Books, 2019.
Identifiers: LCCN 2018043653 (print) | LCCN 2018047298 (ebook) | ISBN 9780825308031 (ebook) | ISBN 9780825308932 (pbk. : alk. paper)
Classification: LCC PS3618.I565 (ebook) | LCC PS3618.I565 A6 2019 (print) | DDC 814/.6—dc23
LC record available at https://lccn.loc.gov/2018043653

For inquiries about volume orders, please contact:
Beaufort Books
27 West 20th Street, Suite 1102
New York, NY 10011
sales@beaufortbooks.com

Published in the United States by Beaufort Books
www.beaufortbooks.com

Distributed by Midpoint Trade Books,
a division of Independent Publishers Group
www.midpointtrade.com
www.ipgbook.com

Printed in the United States of America

Interior design by Mark Karis
Cover Design by Michael Short

FOR THE NEXT GENERATIONS (SO FAR):

Sandolore

Jeff

Bill

Caroline

Jay

Alex

Hollis

Elliott

Silas

and

The Divine Miss P.

TABLE OF CONTENTS

PREFACE

In these days of electronic communications and ephemeral character-limited quips—when we all emerge in public with our eyes focused on the electronic screens in our hands—personal essays seem like a bit of an anachronism. But in a cultural environment full of antagonism, bitterness, and hair-trigger furies, there is value in being able to share in the quiet reflections of others. If we must look down, then, at least, we can spend some time looking inward.

I have always found comfort in reading essays. Their intimacy has reassured and encouraged me to understand that the daily joys and griefs of private life are the real stuff of living—things far removed from the whirl of celebrity and trending news that can so easily sweep our lives into their vortex. Essays, these personal conversations with strangers from other places and other times, have helped me to understand what it means to be human.

Most, if not all of these essays were written for my blog beginning at a time when I had no publication deadlines or other writing commitments. Their sequence here is not entirely chronological; instead, they are arranged to provide some respite from the darkness that was a relentless under-current in these years of my life.

My thanks to my editor, Megan Trank, and publisher, Eric Kampmann for making this book possible; and to Michael Short and Mark Karis, whose designs made it beautiful. I am particularly grateful to my good friend and copy editor, Alicia Manning, for her thorough reading and grammatical rigor. If there are any errors, they are mine.

And finally, my love and gratitude to my brilliant and insightful husband, without whom this book would never have been.

—J. F. Riordan

1

THE SPEED OF TIME

I have been reading Frederick Buechner, who speaks of truth as silence.

I realize how thoroughly I avoid silence. I fear it.

I know now why. Sound is protection. Silence strips away the distraction of noise, revealing old anxieties, regrets, sadness, and pain. Grief resurfaces and tears with sharp nails. These are hard things to embrace.

Instead, I sit on the roof, listening to the tree frogs, the katydids, and the stars, as the breeze blows through the trees, and I hear the truth in their hum and whisper. Not their silence, but mine.

Overhead, clouds whitened by the moon speed past the stars.

My dogs are restless. They smell the threat of coyotes and the enticement of turkeys in the trees nearby.

I sit in awe, humbled by the speed of time in the air.

It is fall now. And life goes past in the wind.

2

LONG GOODBYE

I am lying in bed with 170 pounds of dog: one big, one medium. They are, I regret to admit out loud, in the same proportion in my heart. I do love them both. But the big one, the one who lives inside my soul—he is dying.

Tonight, we did the last thing, a rescue protocol of chemotherapy used only as a last resort. The vet said there was a fifty-fifty chance that it would give him a few more weeks. But no chance that it would save him.

I listen to his breath. The blissful thing is that he doesn't know. Among all the deficits and injustices and hard things of dog life, the one great blessing is not to know your mortality. To him, a hard day is just a hard moment, maybe not an oppressive forever.

Golden retrievers are gentle creatures. They are born sweet. Their docility is not a lack of character, though, as Reggie has demonstrated. He is an artist. His summer days at the lake are not for lounging. They are for a determined and relentless search for the perfect shape, the perfect addition to his sculpture. Tail high and wagging, he scours the floor of the lake with his feet, treading back and forth in a deliberate grid, fully engrossed in his life's work. When he finds what he needs, he pushes it into place with his feet, and dives down to retrieve it, emerging triumphant to the shore with a rock the size of maybe half a soccer ball. He places it on the lawn in his own pattern, discernible only to him. Every morning my husband picks up the rocks, including those stolen from the neighbor's shoreline, and throws them back. But by the end of the day a new work of art—a kind of Reggie Stonehenge—has reappeared.

Struggling to straddle the good days and bad days, to balance his happiness and his pain is my job, watching the progression of the evil cancer, and desperately trying to weigh my needs against his. Trying not to think of my deepest wish—to have him forever—and think only of his—not to suffer. That's all. Just no suffering. No nights in the scary hospital, only nights at home with his people who love him. He doesn't understand if we abandon him, as we did for the surgery on his torn knee. He trembled uncontrollably when we returned to that place for a routine thing.

Among the blessings is the kindness of those who care for him. His vet who returned to the exam room while we waited for blood tests with a flowered quilt to lay on the floor for Reggie and for me; the lab tech who smuggles him extra treats; the oncologist who wraps her arms around him and kisses his face before she begins her work.

We cuddle. I let him lie on the white couch. I rub his

tummy, he puts his head on my shoulder and we comfort one another, as we do. We feed him rotisserie chicken and imported sausage because he will eat it while healthier things go untouched. And who cares? It nourishes him, and he will eat it. It makes him happy. That's all.

This big dog, my puppy dog, at seven weeks used to put his whole self into my arms when he came back inside, and I would hold his small body. He slept on my pillow so I could carry him outside when he stirred. As he grew, he still remembered how to express love in this way, and would lay his massive paws on my shoulders as I knelt next to him, his head towering over mine, his heavy chin on my shoulders. I always held tight, but sometimes distractedly, sometimes hurriedly, sometimes without the same level and intensity of love he had to give me. I had other thoughts. But he always thought about loving me first.

The loss of this love, not human, but canine, may not seem important to everyone. But to me, it is the intimate, personal, and once in my life love of this soul, entrusted to me as a gift I did not deserve or fully appreciate. With all due humility about myself, I wonder if anyone could deserve this trust, this love, this kindness, this full and open heart. Anyone other than another soul like his.

I owe him the most reverent, beloved, happy, and respectful days I can offer him. In his innocence, he is both my king and conscience. He is better than me. And he was born to break my heart.

3

ENGELBERT HUMPERDINCK (THE REAL ONE)

I was just cruising through the music I've collected and came across the final scene from *Hansel and Gretel*'s first act, the "Pantomime." I haven't listened to it in years.

The music begins with the famous "Evening Prayer," which the children sing after their panic at finding themselves alone at night in the Witch's forest. They describe in their prayer the fourteen angels who guard them in their sleep and guide their every step. Gradually, the children fall asleep with their arms around one another. As they sleep—and you can hear it in the music—a mist begins to swirl around and above them, forming a staircase from the Heavens. Fourteen towering angels with enormous wings appear and descend the stairs to the sleeping children. The movement of their wings can be heard as the angels form a circle of protection around the children and take their positions to stand guard over them through the night. Their justice and majesty reverberate. Like the Archangel Michael, who wields his sword against evil, these are warrior angels who do battle in the name of what is right. Their wings are shields, protecting the innocent.

I have always loved that piece of music, and it has particular significance for me because it was an opera my father played for me often when I was a child, and Gretel was my first professional role. I was always grateful that Gretel was sleeping on stage while that music was playing, because I was so moved when I heard it. In fact, I had to distract myself mentally while we sang the prayer duet so that I could sing it without weeping.

I don't think I ever realized, however, until this morning why I find it so. The opera, and Humperdinck, are underappreciated anyway. But that particular section is the most triumphant, profound, and beautiful expression of faith in God's love I know of on earth.

4

WHERE WE ARE NOW

You can't live in a state of emergency forever. Sooner or later, the mundane breaks through, and that's all right. It's the way you cope.

Reggie has mostly good days. His eyes sparkle, and he chases squirrels, and he runs and plays with his dog brother. He has a voracious appetite, and that tells us that he's still feeling okay.

But he is changing. He lies on the floor sometimes and breathes a strange, ragged breath. At first, I was alarmed when I sat beside him to stroke his fur and he made deep resonating rumbles like some prehistoric lizard. But it seems to be pleasure, not pain, and he rolls over and lifts his paw so that his tummy can be rubbed.

Last night, we fell asleep together for a while on the floor, his body—which is about the same size as mine—nestled against me, his breath deep and even as I listened to my own heart pound.

As I sit with Reggie, my mind often returns to the last days and hours I spent with my father, who died of the same disease. He was an affectionate man who loved to be hugged, to hold his daughters' hands. Toward the end, in the haze of the morphine, he cried out when we touched him, afraid someone was trying to kill him. And so in two kinds of agony, his in his deathbed and ours in our helplessness, as I lay on the couch a foot away, he died isolated in the hallucinations of drugs and pain, without my being able to offer any comfort beyond my presence.

Most of the time I try not to think of it.

As we sit near Reggie, sometimes my husband and I look at each other. Did you hear that? Do you think he's okay? And we wonder if we're still doing the right thing. So far, we think we are.

I'm hoping he will tell us.

5

EULOGY FOR MY FATHER

It may seem a little strange to find a Brooklyn boy here in a remote country churchyard. Daddy was a man of sophisticated tastes, well-travelled in the world. As a boy, his mother took him every Saturday to the Metropolitan Opera. In his early years, he rode the subway every day to school. But there was always a rural thread in his life. Brooklyn was farm country in the 1920's, and he spent his summers in Mill Rift, Pennsylvania, a small town with rushing falls and gentle mountains, and during several vacations he worked on a farm.

I have always been proud of Daddy. Proud of his intellect, his accomplishments, and his dignity. I have never known anyone else like him; he knew the answer to every question, he could fix anything, he remembered everything. His interests ranged from science to poetry and music. He is literally the only person I've ever met who read Einstein for fun. When he was recovering from his first major illness, we knew his brain was undamaged when he commented on the Monet print hanging across from his hospital bed.

He was a brilliant engineer, whose inventions advanced

technology, saved lives, and helped in the defense of his country. Above all, he was a man of impeccable integrity. That is a rare thing.

I am indebted to him not just for his love and support of me throughout some of my more wretched moments, but for the gifts he gave me. Almost everything I love in life, I learned from him. From Daddy, I learned to love music and literature, to care about reason and rational thinking, to value education and languages, to be a patriot, and to love freedom, and perhaps most important, I learned my insane passion for dogs. I guess we all did.

He was not a demonstrative man, but he loved to be hugged, and beneath his quiet mask, he was extraordinarily affectionate.

Of all the places he lived, he loved Wisconsin best. I think it was partly because the German culture seemed familiar to him, like the households of his German grandfather and uncle, and partly because he admired the simple integrity of the people here. He liked farmland and the animals, and he saw cities as places that corrupted lives and culture. For all his accomplishments and education, though, he had no pretense or snobbery. He was a good man who lived a simple, honest life. And it seems exactly right that he should rest here, among settlers and veterans, underneath tall trees.

6

IN THE PRAYERS OF A STRANGER

I recently realized that my life had become rather narrow, and that music, once the central focus of my existence, had been reduced to passive listening. So, most days, now, I spend some time playing the piano badly.

It doesn't matter that I can't play as well as I used to when I was serious, just that I play. It is both engaging and mentally clarifying.

To assist in building this new habit, I am using an app that tactfully nudges and rewards for building habits. The app also includes a portion I don't generally use, an opportunity to be part of the app's "community" of people, messaging others who are working on the same things.

These kinds of things are not to my taste. Community means real people that you can see and touch, not invisible strangers. But last night, I casually glanced through this section, and along with the people needing to study for their exams, or lose weight, I came across a message from someone trying to escape an addiction to meth. It was more than a cry for help, it was a howl of despair.

We all live in our little bubbles. We write. We sleep. We go to work. We make dinner. We try to be kind. We are people, presumably, of good will. But then something happens, and the reality of real people in the anguish of suffering and surviving breaks through without warning.

Modern life expands our boundaries beyond our capacity to cope. We are not meant to bear the suffering of the whole world. We are meant to see what is before us and to act. This is why anonymous technology and nonstop news is so hollow and soul-crushing. It puts the suffering of the world before us yet makes us powerless to help. But this was different. It was a stranger in a virtual world, but a voice of such searing pain that it could not be ignored.

So, I wrote. And I prayed. And I wrote that I prayed. And I waited to hear if there would be some response.

There was none. I can contemplate reasons why there was none, but there is not one thing I can do about it.

Disembodied words are no substitute for being present. Maybe there can be some small comfort in being in the prayers of a stranger. But there are some things for which no comfort is possible.

7

PETE LOSES HIS WINGMAN

Pete woke up this morning an only dog. He is an animal with odd pockets of timidity and has depended on Reggie's cheerful steadiness for inspiration to leave the warmth of the house. Normally, when we get up in the still dark mornings, both dogs rush out together. But this morning, Pete wouldn't go. He doesn't like the wind, and he doesn't like the rain. I put on his coat and told him there were squirrels. He wouldn't go. There were no squirrels. Pete isn't stupid, and Reggie wasn't there to encourage him.

We had a rough night last night. Our kind vet and one of his techs came to the house while Pete was locked away upstairs with a very nice bone. We held Reggie and told him we loved him and used something I learned from the late Barbara Woodhouse, an old-school British dog trainer whose advice was of mixed value, but who said that the phrase "What a good dog" had an electrifying effect on dog morale. It was a term with meaning for Reggie, and we said it repeatedly, along with other endearments that are embarrassing for me to admit, but which Reggie seemed to like.

He passed into a deep sleep and was gone. They carried him away. We cried.

Pete wouldn't come down. Pete is our rescue dog. Part whippet, maybe; part pointer, maybe; part lab, maybe. It's a lot of maybe. We call him an Indiana Spotted Dog, because he came from a kill shelter in Indiana. We were told that he was abused, but he's never said anything about it. His disposition is a curious mix of Eeyore and Eddie Haskell, and he is extremely skillful at gaining love, even from strangers. But his courage—and he actually has a great deal—has always been supplemented by the knowledge that he had a larger, eager comrade who was never as fast, but always right behind him. Anyway, in the end, we went up and sat on the bed with Pete, so he wouldn't be alone.

This morning will be the first of many adjustments for Pete. All the bones that are scattered around the yard are his now. He gets both the squeaky squirrel toy and the squeaky frog. There will be no one to steal the thrown tennis ball from; the ball will be for him. He doesn't have to nudge his nose in while someone else is being loved; he gets all the love to himself. He gets both windows when we go for a ride. He won't have to hang around veterinarian waiting rooms to offer moral support. And the two months of gourmet foods—the sautéed chicken livers, the chicken breasts, the raw beef, the Italian sausage—will suddenly cease. It will be back to health food, which is boring, as we all know, but important if you have a future.

We did the right thing. It was hard, but it had to be. I found myself thinking of my late father over the long last days and wishing I could have given him an escape from the agony he was forced to endure from this same disease.

Thank you to all of you who sent us so many words of kindness and support. You can never know how much it meant to us. Pete can't write a thank you. But I think he would if he could. Maybe.

8

IN WHICH MOSES LEADS HIS PEOPLE OUT OF THE WILDERNESS

Dogs grieve. I had heard it and understood it, but I'd never seen it before. We stood in the kitchen talking about Reggie, and hearing the name, Pete's ears perked. I looked him in the eyes and said, "Reggie's gone," and had the uncanny sensation that his face had changed. What did he understand? He had been moping; not eating. He ran outside briefly when necessary and ran right back in. No dawdling in the sun, no sniffling where squirrels had been. He didn't bark when we came home, there was just silence when we opened the door. Pete wasn't in the mood for cheerful greetings, preferring to hide upstairs.

We realized very quickly that none of us could bear the empty silence of the house with Pete hiding and refusing to eat and us feeling our own mortality too much. You get tired of crying, and you can't dwell on death. Another dog was inevitable. We knew, at least, that much.

Since I was a little girl, I have wanted a German Shepherd. I admire them for their bravery and intelligence, their dignity and loyalty. And I think they are beautiful.

But the time had never been right to have a dog who would demand so much training and so much attention. With the passing of Reggie, I realized this was my last chance. In the span of another dog's life, I would probably be too old to have such a powerful dog. And maybe, as much as anything, I couldn't bear having another Golden.

I knew from long correspondence the right person to call, who specialized in traditional, gentle, straight-backed German Shepherds. But the wait would be long. Probably six to twelve months. We sent an email to add our names to the list.

Life-changing things hang upon the large things and the small. And sometimes on the misfortune of others. We all live within some margin of error. At home, we joke about how houses and cars always seem to sense that there's a little extra in the bank, timing their infirmities or demise with the moment when you have something special planned, just as you're about to get ahead. And when you've been saving to buy the German Shepherd puppy you've been waiting for since last year, that's probably about the right time for your furnace to die. And sure enough, within half an hour of applying, we got an email back. "I've just had a cancellation. Would you like to pick him up this weekend?" Somewhere in the universe, someone named Nick has a shiny new boiler for his furnace. But he will wait for another year to get a puppy.

On the other hand, there is Fate. What made us write then? That night? It was too soon; we weren't ready yet.

There aren't many weekends in which we have no obligations, but we had nothing planned. And then there was poor Nick and his furnace.

We got up at 5 a.m. that Saturday morning and made the twelve-hour round trip to an Iowa farm on a dirt road in the middle of nowhere, leaving Pete at home with a friend. It was so remote that the GPS didn't recognize the place. We arrived around noon. Even knowing what I knew about the disposition of these dogs, I was a little nervous about getting out of the car while an extremely large German Shepherd with an enormous head barked at us. But when we met, he gently nudged my hand and then leaned against each of us separately like a big cat. We knew who he was. We had seen his picture on the breeder's website standing shoulder to shoulder with a pony. This was our puppy's uncle. We met the family: Dad, Mom, Grandma, another uncle, a full brother from another litter, and, of course, the puppies.

His official name is Moses, Prince of Egypt. We call him Moses Mooch. He is mostly black, with red legs and paws, and the beginnings of red markings around his face and inside of his ears. He wasn't the biggest puppy in the litter, but he had the longest legs. When we brought him home, he had two floppy ears, like all German Shepherd puppies. This morning he woke up with one standing straight up, the other still flopping at the tip. He looks like a small puppy rabbit.

Moses bounces in with joy. His mother, his father,

and his uncles are gentle giants, so calm and sweet that they make a Golden look like Cujo. He is too young to know about big losses, and he seems delighted to have a new house with a soft blanket and no littermates to eat his dinner. He is curious about sounds. He's not too keen on sleeping alone, but he is getting the hang of it when he must. He likes singing: both his own and others'. He chews hair and the tassels on blankets. He chases ice cubes around the kitchen floor, and has learned to sit when he comes in the house. He's trying really hard not to bite fingers when he plays, although I dreamt the other night that we had a pet crocodile. He has an endearing way of climbing into your lap to snuggle. He has a special affection for the big yellow blanket that probably still smells like Reggie, and from his first moment in the car, he curled up in it and went to sleep.

He's a smart puppy. Today he showed admirable, almost supernatural restraint in resisting the temptation to bite Pete's tail as it hit him repeatedly in the face. You could see his eyes sparkling at the prospect. Pete snarls, though he is just barely tolerant, like a teenager rolling his eyes. But little by little, Moses creeps up on him. Sometimes with a paw on Pete's paw, sometimes copying what Pete is doing, sometimes waiting until Pete is asleep to snuggle up against his back, and sometimes with an insistent puppy bark and a play bow. This morning as we walked, Moses was leaping alongside, trying to bite Pete's floppy ears. We tell Pete that now is the time to make friends, before Moses changes his mind.

The house feels different. There is a puppy bed in the kitchen, and toys on the floor, and half a dozen kinds of large breed puppy food samples in the pantry. We hurry home after work. My husband has notions of the correct number of toys for dogs, but I just buy new ones when I see something he could handle. Moses can't carry most of the ones you see around; they're too big and heavy for puppy teeth.

The juxtaposition of life and death is everywhere always, but it slips in and out of our awareness, sometimes in the background and sometimes in the front. Moses was comforted on his first nights sleeping on the yellow blanket where Reggie closed his eyes for the last time. The puppy trips along behind me to the bird feeder, and I see Reggie's paw prints in the mud. On our visit to the vet for Moses's shots, the tech gently placed a small package on the counter, and while the staff passed around the puppy, I took Reggie out to the car for his last ride home.

Tonight, we all sat on the couch together, and we had to counsel Pete to take note of the dangers of co-sleeping. Moses just barely escaped Pete's indifferent sprawl by climbing onto my lap. Pete seems less than grateful for his new brother, occasionally snarling and sometimes snapping at the puppy. But even so, I think Moses will win out with Pete in the end, even before he gets too big. He's kind of difficult to resist in a force of nature kind of way.

The puppy is sleeping on the rug by my feet. He sleeps hard, indifferent to the sounds of the squirrels chuckling, the geese on the water and the cranes, squawking. He has had a run and eaten as much as he can hold, dancing in excitement while he waited for his bowl. He looks so innocent lying there, probably growing as I watch. I think he's bigger since yesterday, but that's a good thing. He has big boots to fill. And judging from the size of his paws, they might actually fit.

9

LETTER TO A VETERINARIAN

March 5, 2012

Dear Dr. Dave, Julie, Tracy, Matthew, Claudia, and wonderful colleagues:

Please accept our heartfelt thanks for the professionalism, empathy, and care you gave to Reggie during his life and at the very end. We can never fully express how grateful we are for everything you did for him. He was an irreplaceable member of our family. In your every word, every action, you showed how deeply you understand.

Thank you for welcoming Pete when he came along for moral support; for the quilt you lay on the floor for us to lie on as we waited; for the treats; for the genuine affection you and your staff expressed to our dogs. You all helped to make Reggie's short time on earth comfortable, happy, and, ultimately, without fear or pain.

We feel extremely fortunate to know that you are there to continue to care for Pete, and now, for Moses.

We will never forget your many gifts of compassion and kindness.

10

REGRET

My gift to my husband this year was a series of tickets to plays. Our first was this past Saturday, the Milwaukee Rep's *Of Mice and Men.* Since this was my husband's gift, the choice was made to please him, because this is most definitively not my kind of story.

I was an English major, and I read a lot, as you might imagine. (I should also point out that I am of an age in which English majors actually read literature. No, seriously. It was something that was required.) But somehow, I had managed my whole life never to read *Of Mice and Men.* I suppose we all have gaps in our educations, but this was an intentional one. I knew instinctively that I would feel bad reading this book, and I hate feeling bad. In fact, I spend a great deal of effort and energy working on feeling good. I knew vaguely that Lennie was mentally challenged, but I was content to leave my information level there.

So (spoiler alert, for those of you whose education gaps are similar), when they shot the dog in the first act, I had a pretty clear idea of where we were headed. Recognizing foreshadowing is an English-major thing. My husband, who watched me uneasily out of the corner of his eye during pretty much the entire play, said later that he was fully prepared for me to break out in noisy sobs when they killed the dog. He was holding his breath about what might happen at the end. To me, I mean, not to the characters. He, literate, cultured, and urbane creature that he is, had actually read the book.

Curiously, I was utterly dry-eyed throughout the entire play. This is not typical of me, since, as my family never lets me forget, I cried at the end of the sailboat race in *Stuart Little.* But I have been thinking about *Of Mice and Men* for three days now.

I have been wondering about George; wondering about the choice he made. Could he come to terms later with the relief he must have felt? Could he forgive himself for what he did, even though he did it to spare his friend pain and terror? Did he go on to fulfill the dream he had carried so long in his wanderings? If so, was he able to find joy in it? Or was it poison-filled?

Living with your choices—without regret—is a difficult thing. But perhaps regret is the right thing, and our souls require it.

11

LOST YOUTH

People have been asking me about Pete. How is he? Has he adjusted to life with his enormous brother? And so, lest anyone think that a youthful, high-energy German Shepherd has completely stolen the show, a word about our smaller, auxiliary dog.

Pete is now officially the old man of the family. His white face and love of the couch are in contrast with his youthful self, who leapt and ran like the coursing hound whose blood is somewhere in his veins. He loved to run, and when he soared over a low-lying bush to give chase to some trespassing creature, he looked exactly like the image on the side of a bus.

He rarely shows this side of himself now. He eyes the antics of Moses and his puppy friend with an air of skepticism, occasionally joining in the chase, but only briefly. But he is just as likely to bark and chase them down, rolling them onto their backs as he shows his teeth, just to show who's boss. Remarkably, Moses, who outweighs him nearly two to one, rolls over timidly, submitting to Authority.

Pete is a snuggler. When he sleeps with us in the bed, I will frequently wake up to find his face lying delicately against my cheek. He is difficult to budge in the mornings, preferring warm blankets to a brisk excursion in snow and cold. If you are busy and not paying him proper attention, he will nudge your hand with his nose, insisting that you pet him, even if your hand has a cup of hot coffee or some good bourbon in a hand-blown glass.

There aren't many photos of Pete, but this is because he has a horror of cameras. We don't know much about Pete's early life, because he came to us at 10 months old, or so. We know it wasn't entirely happy, and we also know that it involved something bad with cameras. When a camera comes out, Pete slinks away or hides under the table. In the photos we do manage to take, Pete's expression conveys the idea that he's in a hostage situation. iPhones seem to have made a difference but haven't completely eliminated the problem. I think maybe it's the high-pitched hum of digital flashes. My husband believes someone posted an unflattering picture of Pete on Facebook.

In this unusually cold winter, both dogs have been getting less exercise than they should. Our daily walks in the woods after work have been curtailed by sub-zero temperatures and early darkness. I love these walks as much as they do, but the dogs are able to run more easily than I in the deep snow of the woods. Pete, on the trails, becomes his old self, with Moses trailing behind, not slowly, but less agilely and with a higher center of gravity.

The other day, they both started at the chuffing snorts of deer nearby, and in a split second they took off to give chase, Pete in the lead, and Moses leaping behind. They were gone for nearly five minutes, and I ignored it, knowing the deer were safe, that the dogs would be doubly tired when they returned. After a reasonable period of time, and before they made it to the next county, I whistled for them, and I heard them charging back long before I could see them.

This is our routine, and in it, Pete and I return to our younger days while Moses simply blows off steam. The dogs bounce back to the car, panting, snow-covered and happy, and then, in my own tribute to lost youth, we go up the road a bit to practice bootleg turns in the snowy parking lot of the golf course.

You have to make your own fun.

12

LAST DAY NORTH OF THE TENSION LINE

Today is my last day on Washington Island. The ferry leaves tomorrow at 8 am, and we'll be on it.

Normally, I like to walk the deck and chat with the crew, but the dogs are with me, and there's something about the ferry ride that scares them. So, we sit together in the car, and I talk and sing to them. They like that, and they usually sing along. Pete, who is undoubtedly the coward in the family, is mostly unbothered by the motion, but Moses is. When we hit the ice fields, the noise frightens them both and they tremble. It seems to get worse each trip.

Last night, I walked home from a dinner party in the dark with the wind screaming from the lake. Its noise and power were awesome—in the old-fashioned sense of the word. The dogs leapt with joy to see me, and we went out again to hear the wind and look at the moon and the clouds. They ran ahead of me through the snow, sniffing at deer tracks. The wild remoteness of the Island is oddly comforting to me, and I feel safer here than anywhere else on earth, even when the wind leaps and howls as if it would tear us off the ground and spin us into space.

I like to say I live in exile from Washington Island, and most people think it's a joke. But leaving this place tears at me, and even though I will be happy to be home again, a part of myself will be missing.

13

MAYBE ICARUS WAS A TURKEY

We live at Turkey Central. It started out small a few years ago, when we would occasionally hear turkey calls in the spring. But now there are turkeys—about forty of them—who roost in our trees every night, and their comings and goings are part of the rhythm of our days. At dawn and at dusk, you can look up into the tops of the trees and see these unwieldy, bulbous creatures, precariously perched on the tiniest of branches, fifty feet above the floor of the woods. I have no idea how they manage to stay there, but so far, I have seen no evidence of them falling. They make quite a lot of noise, too, which I rather enjoy.

For those pedants among you, I draw your attention to the fact that wild turkeys constitute a flock. Domestic turkeys constitute a rafter, or a gang.

I don't know.

One of my great pleasures in life is to watch the turkeys at dusk, flying, one by one, up to their nighttime berths. They gobble as they make a running start, with a long rumble like a B-52 at takeoff, and then, unexpectedly, they take to the air, and with a great flapping, land on a perfectly unsuitable branch, bobbling back and forth, as they establish their balance. This takes some time, and it is most enjoyable to watch with a cocktail in hand. Preferably bourbon, but I am not always particular.

We frequently attempt to bore our guests with it, but everyone who witnesses it seems as riveted as we are.

Last year, we had one turkey who broke the routine. Instead of using the little hill in the woods for his launch, he would courageously mount the big hill to our house, where dogs do dwell. He would get almost to the top, near the patio, and then he would turn and run down the hill, his wings flapping, using the hill for acceleration on takeoff. My husband commented on it one night in amazement, and after that, the turkey came—this one bird, alone—every night.

I came to think of this bird as an innovator, a cultural leader, possibly breaking the Darwinian bonds of avian technology. I looked for him, I admired him, and I was delighted by him. Then came turkey season. I don't hunt, so I don't know what the rules are about where you can shoot, or when, or how. But I can say that the number of turkeys was considerably diminished. As winter came on, there were only about a dozen left. And our innovator was gone. The flock that remained continued its old habits, without variety or novelty.

In my heart, I know what probably happened. But I like to think of him, laboriously climbing the perilous hill, alone, undaunted, his vision of glory before him, as he turns and begins the run to takeoff, lifting up exultantly from the earth, closer and closer to the sun, on his way to immortality.

It's spring again, and we have more turkeys than ever. But not the innovator. The flock has lost some of its magic for me.

He was a turkey. And I think of him every day.

14

IN PRAISE OF SMALL TOWNS

A writer in a national magazine recently theorized that small town voters who are worried about the deterioration of American culture are "insular," and unenlightened, stuck in the past, resistant to progress.

Having grown up in a small town, and also having taught at a high school in the inner city of Milwaukee, I can say that most of my students and their families were also living in their hometown, and the hometown of their families. Does that make them insular? Or does it make them normal?

City life is fine. It is filled with cultural, social, and employment opportunities that may not exist elsewhere. You can choose how and whether to connect with other people. But bustle is not for everyone, nor is anonymity.

Some of us choose to live in a different way. But it would be a mistake to believe that small town life is a bucolic and peaceful existence. Living in a small community is not for the faint of heart.

Small towns are a microcosm of the human experience,

but with more intensity. You live shoulder to shoulder with your oldest friends, and your fiercest enemies. Daily, you encounter the person who cheated you; who stood you up; who broke your heart. And the people who know your complete history: every bad decision, every embarrassment, every moment of kindness (if any). In cities, there can be the relief of some anonymity, but not in a small town. Living in a small town is a psychologically raw way to live.

But small town life also requires a deep connection to community that city people may not acquire. It often means that you go to church because that is what is expected and how decent people behave. It means you are surrounded by people who know you. In the city, it's called networking. In a small town, the network is your neighbors, and you are expected to participate. Your neighbors are the ones who gather around you to celebrate births and mourn deaths. They plow your driveway when you have the flu. They raise money to help in a tragedy. They put an arm around your shoulder. They make casseroles. And you, in turn, celebrate, and mourn, and plow, and comfort, and bake. This sharing and mutual support is as old as human beings. And it is good.

The cultural gatekeepers promulgate the notion that someone who doesn't live in your community can decide what's wrong with you and what you need. It's an insult and a barely veiled one. We are flyover country: insular, irrelevant bumpkins filled with prejudices, unsuited to participate in the enlightened progressivism of the cities, destined never to be famous. Living in a small town means that you are aware of the scorn heaped upon you by city dwellers who think they are better, and you shrug your shoulders and get on with it.

Maybe resisting progress isn't all bad. In an age of celebrity and reality television, of Instagram and Twitter, most small-town people live out quiet, uncelebrated lives of dignity and depth. They work; they care for their families and their friends; they are kind; they mow their lawns and mop their floors. They may not be famous or trend-setting. But they have lives worth living.

And that is something worth standing for.

15

THE FAITH OF JUSTINE

I almost had a student whose life I changed. But she changed mine instead.

She came into my high school Speech class on the first day of a soggy August afternoon and sat in the front row. She was quiet and serious, and she didn't seem to have a lot of interaction with the other students. She wore the thickest set of glasses I have ever seen. And I realized almost immediately that she sat in the front because she could see almost nothing.

She was an eager student who came to class, joined in discussions, did her work, and clearly wanted to learn. She was highly intelligent and motivated. I didn't realize at first that she also eagerly wanted to be in mainstream classes with her peers. But that was not to be.

A few weeks after school had started she was removed from my class, and Justine came to ask my help. The administration—a good one, by the way—had determined that she should be in another class that would be more helpful to her. Justine wanted to be in my class. I wanted that, too.

I did what I could, but we lost that battle. And maybe we should have. I'm still not really sure. But I do know now that even if it was the wrong decision, it was not enough to stop her.

I lost track of Justine. I left teaching to do other work, and she went on with her education. I heard of her now and then. She was at a private university and doing well. She was a member of a society run by and for the visually impaired and was an advocate for their work.

Years passed, and one day I met Justine at a banquet for the society she belonged to. She didn't remember me. But the next day, she sent an email apologizing. She couldn't see my face, and in the noise of the banquet hall she couldn't hear my voice well enough. But now she remembered. As I do with all the former students who contact me, I invited her to lunch.

I picked her up at her public housing apartment, silently worrying about her safety there. Justine described for me her passion to help the poorest of the poor in Africa. She told me of her missionary visits to Africa, of her plans for her master's degree, of the small consulting firm she started to assist with the work she dreamed of doing. She was leaving in a few weeks for Washington D.C. to do a fellowship.

Her vision was worsening. All she could see now were hazes of light and, if she turned her head a certain way, a small window of fuzzy images. She spoke about how difficult it is to function in an unknown place without the ability to see what's around her. What was in the shadows? Was it something about to fall on her? A curb? A dangerous insect? Someone lurking in the dark to harm her?

Justine told me that if she wanted to, she could imagine in the darkness that there were dragons, and insects, and poisonous snakes. She could see dangers around her everywhere and all the time. But she chose, she said, to imagine other things: tall trees; flowers blooming; sunlight; and gentle creatures. Armed with these images, she goes alone into the darkest corners of the world and manages to survive. She seeks these journeys, and she seems to require them.

Listening to her speak, I realized that faith is not just about a belief in God. It is about the stories we tell ourselves when we are in the dark.

I have lost touch with Justine again, but her steady vision has stayed with me over the years. When I quaver in my incredibly easy life, I think of her somewhere in the dangerous world with only a cane to help her: patiently, quietly, and with unimaginable grit, making her way through the darkness, seeing only beauty all around her.

This is the faith of Justine. It is a stronger and richer faith than most of us could ever possess. The curse of her circumstances created the necessity, but it is the quality of her character that made it into a great and unwavering gift.

16

THE NOSTALGIA OF CROWS

I am a crow lover.

I had never seen a crow until I moved to Wisconsin in my childhood, and I remember being astonished at how big they were. I first noticed them in the spring when their big, clumsy fledglings would fall off their perches onto their beaks and would make odd, baby caws that were laughably unbeautiful. But their parents were sleek and affectionate, and there seemed to be large families of mothers and fathers and aunts and uncles.

We fed them. My mother would leave them meat scraps and suet. They would gather in the early mornings and winter evenings, circling overhead and calling. It was rare to see one alone. Most often, though, they would travel in pairs. Nordic myth says that they were the messengers of the god, Odin, and they always seem to carry both mystery and omen.

When I grew older, my brother gave me a crow call, and I would use it to summon them. They almost always responded, and we would carry on conversations in a language that consisted on my side merely of imitation. I can't say what was intended on their side.

Crows are very intelligent. I remember reading somewhere that there was a man who somehow rescued a baby crow, and from that day on, the entire flock (technically, I believe, a murder of crows) would greet him in his car every day as he entered his subdivision, and escort him to the main road when he left. They always remembered his heroism, although, perhaps, it was a tribute that not everyone would appreciate.

Somehow, bleak winter days—the days with neither sun nor snow—seem like crow days, and today was one of those days. As I was hurrying in from my car to a meeting, I heard in the distance the rough song of crows, and it flashed me back to my childhood, ambling home from school through the snow, cawing and calling to the birds who seemed to know me.

I realized at once how much I have missed them, and I have resolved to go back to carrying my crow call in my pocket.

17

SING

We went to see a world premier play at the Milwaukee Rep last night: *American Song* by Joanna Murray-Smith. It was beautifully written and moving, and performed by only one actor, the talented James Devita, whose career I have been following since we were both students in Milwaukee. It was a powerful theatrical experience about which I have only one quibble. But this is not a theatrical review blog, and what matters is that you should go, if you can. You will weep.

But what actually came away with me on the deepest level, former English major that I am, was the long and loving reference to Walt Whitman.

This sounds a little silly, but I had forgotten about Walt Whitman.

I grew up reading Walt Whitman, often, and with gradually increasing understanding. At first, I just loved the rhythms of the poetry. I was carried along by his passion. Then I fell in love with what it was.

I am annoyed by people who ask: "What is the poet trying to say?" My slightly irritable answer is: "He's not *trying* to say anything. He's saying it. The poem is what he says."

And this is why imbuing art with a message which is not intrinsically involved in the art itself can be dangerous. But Whitman was not delivering a message. He was writing poetry. The poetry is the message. At least, it is if it's done well.

I taught Whitman's poetry as a high school American Lit teacher. And even now, I am a great—possibly overly enthused—re-reader of many things. But Walt Whitman has not entered my thoughts for too many years now, and last night I re-encountered him with a fresh heart.

The play quotes a line from "Leaves of Grass," in which the songs of people in different lives sing out in their own voices to make the joyous melody of freedom, of individual value and dignity: *Each singing what belongs to him or her and to none else…singing with open mouths their strong melodious songs.* I loved that Murray-Smith celebrated that celebration of America.

Pali, the poetry-writing ferry captain in my books, is a man who sings songs, whose work vibrates with a unique and beautiful voice. The question is: whose voice is it?

The mysteries of life delight me.

18

AN INAUSPICIOUS BEGINNING

Today was one of those days. Generally, I try to remind myself that all my problems are lucky people problems. But sometimes, you have to allow yourself a tiny bit of self-pity.

I arrived at the office, dressed for a long day of back-to-back meetings. Since I usually start early, I eat my breakfast at my desk. I am fortunate to have a beautiful office in an historic building with oriental carpet, oil paintings, and a brass chandelier. But underneath my desk, in a concession to practicality, is one of those plastic sheets that allow your office chair to roll on carpet. I should note that, for once in my life, I was wearing (relatively) sensible shoes, a pair of low-heeled black sandals, but with, as it turns out, very slippery soles. I was carrying my bowl of yogurt and blueberries in one hand, and my café au lait in the other, and had just stepped behind my desk, when my foot slid out from under me. In what seemed like slow motion, I went down, my hands went up, and a cascade of yogurt, blueberries, and café au lait went up into the air in a spectacular arcing curve, landing, with rather remarkable accuracy, on my head. My

Italian designer suit jacket sleeves were soaked through with coffee, my hair was clinging to my forehead, and there were blueberries kind of mushed into the part of the oriental carpet that wasn't covered by the plastic sheet thing. The receptionist called from downstairs to ask if we had knocked over a file cabinet. "No," I said. "That was me." My colleague from across the hall tried to be helpful by laughing and bringing paper towels. After going through a massive stack of paper towels, in a triumph of optimism over yogurt, I went to one of my female colleagues who had just arrived and asked her if I was presentable enough. She paused for a moment as she looked me over." I think you need to change."

I went home to start again and missed my first meeting.

I suppose, in some respects, it was the highlight of the day.

19

WHAT'S UNDER MY DESK

There are all kinds of interesting ways for authors to communicate with their readers and with one another. On one site, authors are asked to post photos of where they write and compose a little essay about it. Don't tell my publicist, but I haven't done that yet. Still, I couldn't help feeling as if I should post this edition, not of where I write, but of what's under where I write.

At the moment, we are in the midst of post-construction landscaping, and maybe the sound of the bulldozer is scary. For whatever reason, Moses, who is always nearby anyway, is unusually close. I am writing with his head on my feet, and his ears pressed up against my knees. It's kind of nice, actually.

20

THE PERILS OF PUBLIC MUSIC

There used to be a lot of mockery about Muzak, that bland public music that took popular tunes like "I Can't Get No Satisfaction," removed the drums, and added violins and a zither. Its mediocrity was intended to soothe, but for people who actually like music, it served mostly to irritate. I don't know if Muzak still exists. But if the corporate entity has faded, its inane heritage carries on with a vengeance.

Public music wears on the nerves. Airlines have decided that their passengers want to hear it as they get on and off the plane. Perhaps they believe that the hostilities taking place as passengers hunt for space to stow their carry-ons will be somehow mitigated by jazz. Unwilling to participate in this ritual combat, I always check my bags, take my seat as quickly as possible to get out of the scrum, and have the leisure to watch what's going on around me. I admit to being amused by the contrast between the activities just overhead and the saxophone music. If the music is an attempt to create the impression that everyone's having a good time, it's a fail. But maybe the airline executives have a previously unsuspected sense of humor.

Hotels play music in their public spaces, and the selections are clearly chosen to set the correct tone of "fashionableness" and "chic." At the last place I stayed—iced-in while the airport was closed for two days—the effect was surreal. A colleague described it as "Bollywood on acid." Even at four in the morning, during a discussion with the desk clerk over whether the gym was open, the empty lobby resonated with a strange undulating sound that created a vague feeling of nausea.

In the public rooms outside of a conference, the tinkling sound of wind chimes and synthesized chanting interferes with serious thinking and creates a mental discord between the reality of work and the unattainability of vacation.

At resort hotels, the soothing sound of surf is covered up by the incessant beat of techno-funk amplified at the beach. Inside the hotel lobby, however, you can hear the sound of waves, but only embedded in the Tibetan chimes of corporate spa music.

Travel, particularly business travel, is stressful. You are away from home and family and dogs. The TSA has put its hands all over your self and your stuff. Your feet hurt. You packed for the wrong climate. You haven't finished writing your speech when the leading expert on the topic will be on the panel. Your flight is delayed, and you may miss a conference call with your boss. Your cell phone battery is low. You are breathing stale air from planes, airports, and hotel conference rooms. You're eating unhealthy food, and the gym was closed when you tried to work out. The airport announcements blare at you, and neon signs invite you to eat bad things, and spend money on stuff you don't really need. At times like these, you need your thoughts to yourself. So, a word to people who control the volume: just turn it off.

Please.

21

REAL COOK KITCHEN

My husband and I recently changed our cable service, and suddenly, after years of watching TV only for Packers' games, election nights, and storm coverage (we live in the Midwest), we have TV's in three different rooms, and I am watching nearly every night. DVR technology is nothing new to most Americans, but to me, it is an exciting new arena for experimentation. Gone is the slightly stuck-up tone I used to use when I'd say in response to someone's query about a great new show: "We hardly ever watch TV."

In short, I have been watching a lot of cooking shows. Actually, only one: Ina Garten, the Barefoot Contessa. I adore her and want to be her friend. Although, for the record, someone who cares about her should take her aside and suggest that she rely a little less on stock phrases lest she descend into self-parody like Martha Stewart. But I digress.

As I am fast-forwarding through my DVR'd shows (I also adore *Top Gear*, the British version, and am already heartily sick of *Rehab Addict*), I have had occasion to pick up the tail ends and the very beginnings of other cooking shows, and gradually, I have been slowing down to watch these brief parts of them. It's fascinating how many chefs and/or cooks with widely varying styles one can find. There was a time when Americans had only one beloved television chef: Julia Child. But now, we have as many as the Food Channel can program.

What intrigues me most are the formal methods of these TV cooks, even as they, apparently, revel in their idiosyncrasies. They may be ranchers' wives, or girls who dress up in costumes to match their menus, or people who have very tight budgets, but their ingredients are mise en place, their kitchens are carefully organized, and everything always goes smoothly. They always have the ingredients they need and the right size pan.

This is not an accurate reflection of the cooking adventure. At least not in my house.

Let me begin with my stove. It is a vintage Chambers stove from somewhere in the 1950's. It is lined with firebrick, and weighs about 600 pounds. I got it for free 23 years ago and shipped it to Wisconsin from Maryland.

I know.

Anyway, this stove has become a strange part of my identity. It is special, and mostly wonderful. The rusty burners are infinitely adjustable and have different configurations for different kinds of cooking. There's a stove top broiler with a griddle on top and a well, a kind of mini oven, which I may have used once. One of the things I love about my stove is that there is no electronic anything on it. This means that even in a power outage I can make a cup of tea or a lovely beef stew to eat in front of the fire. We've lived in our current house for 13 years and had approximately three power outages. But never mind.

The other identifying characteristic of my stove is that it has no oven thermostat. Apparently—and I hadn't realized this until he told me some months later—when my late, adored, engineer father re-installed the stove in our new house, he decided for some reason that the thermostat was dangerous. Or something. Anyway, he removed it.

We won't get into my father's approach to repair. I'll save that for another day.

But in the aftermath, when I was complaining that my oven either burned or undercooked things, no matter how I set the temperature, the subject of the thermostat came up. After pondering this problem for some weeks, I casually mentioned to my mother that it was probably time for me to get a new stove. "But you can't!" she exclaimed, horrified. "Your father worked on that stove for two whole days. He would be so hurt!"

This line has become a source of, at first, teasing and, now, resignation for my husband. When I mention that in our kitchen renovation we should consider getting a new stove, he points out that we can't because my father—now gone for nearly six years—worked on the stove, and it is now historic. I used to think this was funny.

But, anyway, this is one reason that cooking in my house is not like the cooking on TV.

The other reason is me. I'm actually a pretty good cook. I learned the art of creative cooking from my mother, who all her life made delicious meals by artfully tossing in a bit of this and a handful of that—all accompanied by copious quantities of butter and good white wine—but whose techniques were somewhat erratic. My mother rarely used a measuring cup, and when she did, it was only a gesture.

I learned the need for method in cooking from my 6th grade home economics teacher, Mrs. Wallesverd. Mrs. Wallesverd was old school in every sense. She was the kind of teacher who brooked no nonsense, and who looked at you in a disapproving way if you strayed from the path. Those looks had a powerful effect. But cooking is chemistry, after all, and I learned from her why sifting flour mattered, but also why you wash the glasses and silverware first, and other key points of organized housewifery. Another topic for the future: the serious loss to children in the elimination of home economics courses.

So my cooking is a curious amalgam of creativity and method, and except for those days when the oven temperature isn't quite right—which, I must admit, are rather frequent—it usually turns out rather well.

On Thanksgiving morning, I decided to make pumpkin bread. Bread, as you probably know, requires baking. Which requires an oven. Which, unless you are a French chef with a traditional boulangerie, usually requires a thermostat.

Nevertheless, emboldened by the success of my pies yesterday, I decided to give it a try. Quite apart from anything else, the kitchen in our old house is cold, and the oven heats things up nicely. It's the firebrick.

I have discovered that by pushing in on the alleged temperature gauge as it turns, I can usually alter the temperature of the oven up or down. But only generally up, or generally down. Never so specifically as, say, 350 degrees. It's all a crap shoot. So, I turned on the gas, listened for the sound of it rushing through the burners, and inserted my little plastic igniter into the hole in the oven. A sort of a WHOOMP sound told me that the oven was lit.

It's all an adventure.

It was while I was doing this, and pulling together the ingredients, that I was struck by how completely unlike a television show my cooking was. Now, I know from Mrs. Wallesverd that level teaspoons are important in baking, and I also know that if I don't put everything out and premeasure, I will forget something. That's like a cooking show. But that's pretty much where the resemblance ends.

I have never seen a cooking show chef peer into her flour canister and discover that it's empty. Nor have I seen her have to open a bag of flour and have to deal with the mess as it poufs out of the paper package all over the counter and floor. Television chefs don't have to interrupt their cooking to rinse out the flour canister and dry it because the rim has something crusty on it, and it's probably not a great idea to put a new bag of flour in it without washing it first.

Cooking show chefs have the right size pans carefully laid out. They rarely have to sit down on the cold kitchen floor to rummage through the pan cabinet, searching for the right size. There is no avalanche of colanders when they pull out the possibilities. They don't run out of paper towels and have to run down to the basement for another roll.

They don't have bread pans purchased on the run at Piggly Wiggly that were intended 23 years ago to be temporary but have endured ever since with no sign of a Williams Sonoma replacement. They don't have to dig around for their reading glasses and then hold said pans under the light to see if, somewhere, they have their dimensions imprinted on them. "That's probably about eight inches, isn't it?"

Rarely are TV chefs reduced to pulling a tape measure out of the drawer (conveniently stored in the kitchen to resolve extemporaneous remodeling inspirations) to measure their pans. Television chefs never lick their fingers. Nor the beaters of their mixers. They never have to interrupt themselves to throw the ball for the puppy, and then have to wash their hands again so that their pumpkin bread doesn't have puppy spit as a flavoring, which is undesirable, no matter how engaging the puppy.

Television chefs remember to plug in the mixer before they try to turn it on, and their whisk attachment doesn't have one broken wire that makes an ungodly racket when it hits the sides of the bowl.

Television chefs also don't have to open the oven and then discover that the hardware store thermometer has once again overturned itself, and has to be fished out from the bottom of the oven, while carefully avoiding the burn from yesterday's similar adventure, and then curse the designer of the thermometer who thought it would be a good idea to make a little clip for the thermometer which serves only to make it impossible to move it, but not to actually make it stay in place when someone is trying to put a pan in or take it out.

I was reflecting on all these things as I bumbled around, making bread, relishing my time in my kitchen, sipping my café au lait, and licking my fingers. There were all kinds of birds on the bird feeder outside the kitchen window and deer browsing in the snowy woods below the house. My husband was still sleeping and later, when he woke up, the house would smell of good things and the kitchen would be warm. So, not so much like television chef cooking, but much more satisfying and real—a truly happy morning.

I have to stop now. The timer just went off. The one that only works occasionally.

And the pumpkin bread smells delicious.

Irony Alert: As I should have realized, had I not been lured into oven complacency by the success of my pies and bread, the reason the baking went so well was because the oven was keeping its temperature low. But this is not the right temperature for roasting a turkey. Especially not a larger than usual turkey.

22

THE ISLAND

The novels in my series, North of the Tension Line, are set on Washington Island, Wisconsin. The passage to Green Bay between the tip of the peninsula and the Island is one of the most dangerous in the Great Lakes, and many ships have gone down there. The French explorers called it *Portes des Mortes*. The Door of Death.

Probably, it is my yearning for rest and escape that has led me to seek out remote locations whose isolation creates the refreshing sensation of having fallen off the edge of the earth. Washington Island is that kind of place.

I have come to know Washington Island well. The Northern Lights are a common sight there, and it is small enough that the waves of Lake Michigan can be heard almost everywhere. It was visited in the 17th century by the great French explorer and fur trader Robert de LaSalle, and its culture is still influenced by the many Icelandic immigrants who came there in the 19th century. With a population of fewer than 400 residents, the interactions of civilization in all its complexities of affection and animosity are intensified by the lack of options. When winter comes, those 400 people are your friends, your enemies, and your salvation. My books are a loving, but mostly unromantic tribute to that way of life. The title is a reference to the island's unofficial slogan.

Washington Island really is north of the tension line. People almost universally describe the experience of crossing the water to the Island as having all the stresses of the world fall away.

One of my favorite places there is the Albatross, a little hamburger stand in downtown Washington Island—and by downtown I mean the intersection where there are four buildings comprising the Albatross, the post office, recently for sale, a charming old house, and what appears to be an abandoned building but which, I have been told, is a repair shop. I'm not sure what is repaired there, but it certainly is not the building.

Anyway, at the Albatross, the slogan is "WE ARE NOT FAST. We are good. We are cheerful. But we are not fast. If you want fast, go to Chicago. But north of the tension you are, so relax."

Chicago and its citizens are a major source of tourism revenue in Door County—so it's a little unfair to make fun of them as much as everyone does. But it's always entertaining.

When I was on the Island a month or so ago, I was chatting with the proprietor of the general store, and he told me that a tourist had been in recently—I like to think it was someone from Chicago—and with map in hand had asked him: "Can you show me where to find the tension line?"

We laughed—because, let's face it, it's fun to laugh at tourists, especially, as in my case, when you're one yourself—but the truth of the matter is that we are all carrying our own little tension lines, and sometimes we are not all that great at escaping them. We need as much help as we can get.

Life on the Island, though, is clearly not for everyone. If you have AT&T cellular service, by the way, forget it. You may as well just leave your phone at home. There are restaurants—nothing fancy, mind you—a grocery store, the Mercantile, which is a combination hardware store, furniture showroom and gift shop, and a place that sells liquor and shoes, repairs appliances, and is affectionately known to Islanders as Shoes and Booze.

Washington Island does not have the tourist cachet of, say, Mackinac Island. In fact, the economy is rather tenuous. There are horses, I suppose, but no carriages. And there's not much in the way of shopping. But it does have this splendid isolation which is both alluring and a little bit terrifying. You'd better not nick an artery with a fishing knife or have a heart attack while you're there. The main hospital is 90 miles away in Green Bay, and it's a wait for the helicopter to get to you.

I think, actually, that it's this mix of hardship and natural beauty that creates the irony in the title of my book, but in any case, while I am writing about being there, I can pretend that I am there, and I have an excuse to return there on a regular basis.

It's not life in paradise, but it's as close as I need to get.

23

SIGNS OF LIFE

In Wisconsin, snowdrops normally bloom in March and, true to their name, burst through remnants of snow. This year, the only snow left is what has been plowed into mountains at the edges of driveways and parking lots, and even those are nearly gone.

But the snowdrops are here all the same, though rather early. And none the less welcome for that.

I'd rather have flowers than almost anything. Except, perhaps, snow.

24

LAST PEONIES

It's been a lousy spring. I loved the harsh cold and daily snow of the winter, even while everyone else was complaining. But this spring, even by Wisconsin standards, has been just plain bad: cold, rainy, and miserable. June is nearly gone, and we haven't yet felt the full bloom of summer. It's oppressive, and it feels like a year lost from one's life.

I adore peonies. I recall one summer day, coming into the kitchen of my much-beloved German voice coach to find a full vase of deep red peonies. They took my breath away with their beauty. Noticing my reaction, my coach said to me, "They are like Wagner, aren't they?"

That was a long time ago, in another lifetime. My peonies, which are abundant and in many colors, are the joy of my every June. I adore their perfume, and their variety, and I pick them extravagantly to fill the house. But this year, I have been distracted and busy, and I missed almost all their bloom. This evening, after my early-rising husband had gone to bed, the dogs and I went out into the summer twilight—mercifully dry—and picked the last remaining blossoms. I tried not to notice the petals on the ground, wasted by the rain, and the browning and withered blooms that still remained on the stems. I found a few lovely and fully blossoming flowers, and I cut them all to bring into the house. Despite there being so few, their scent fills the room.

Normally, I am jealous of my flowers, and I find it difficult to part with them. But this time, I know that my peonies will sleep only tonight in my house. Tomorrow, I will bring them to my mother's bedside for her to savor their scent and the voluptuousness of their color. However much I try to pretend otherwise, I know she will not be here when they bloom again. I dread to think of seeing peonies for the last time. I hope she doesn't know.

25

EULOGY FOR MY MOTHER

We are a family of eccentrics: artists, inventors, writers, dreamers, and rabble rousers. There is no doubt that Mom was smart, but she was a practical person, and our intellectual interests probably come from our late father. But our passion, our intuition, and our love for a battle came from our mother.

She was a vibrant, enthusiastic, and extraordinarily difficult woman. And let's be honest: she took great pride in being difficult.

Two weeks ago, she fell. I got the call around midnight the night before I was scheduled to leave for a week-long business trip. I went to her house. The paramedics had already left. They had wanted to take her to the hospital for stitches. She was bruised, cut, and bloody, but next to her bed was the form she had signed refusing treatment. She was determined to stay in her own house, but I decided that she could not stay alone and made arrangements for 24-hour companionship. The next night, on Monday in D.C., I got a call from the agency. My mother was refusing to allow the caregiver in her house, and on her walker, she had a loaded Smith and Wesson. For the people involved, it was shocking. But to me, it was just business as usual with Ethel.

My mother's old friend Rose remarked the other day on my mother's fierce loyalty. Ethel didn't like everyone. She was not especially warm and fuzzy, she was outspoken to a fault, and she was highly capricious in her tastes. But once you were her friend, you were her friend forever. I think the greatest hurts my mother felt were those by people from whom she had expected the same kind of loyalty she offered.

My mother loved to laugh. She was playful. She loved to dance. She loved to be out among people. In this way, she was an odd match to my father, who was quiet and reserved, and who liked to sit at home and read. But they both loved to dance, and their dance of choice was the Polish hop, which, if you know my mother, is perfect because it involves a lot of foot stomping. My brother and sister talk about their childhood, before I was born, sitting in their pajamas at the top of the stairs at one of our parents' regular parties. They and their friends would roll back the rugs on the living room floor and the house would shake with the vibrations of couples dancing and stomping for hours on end. It was this same group of friends who had costume parties. Most memorably was the one in which my parents dressed up as Talos and Terrier missiles—the ones for which my father was developing guidance systems at the time. My mother's had a pair of pretty legs in red high heels peeking out at the bottom. I keep the photo at my desk.

My father's family were first- and second-generation immigrants. His father was born in County Cork. But it was my mother who had the Irish temperament. It was through Mom that we can trace our English ancestors to the founding of Harvard and to the American Revolution. It will surprise no one who knew her that she came from those lawless rabble-rousers, the Green Mountain Boys, who were with Ethan Allen when he took Fort Ticonderoga and fought later at Bunker Hill and the Battle of Bennington. Ethel was a fighter.

But she was also a giver. One of my earliest memories is going with my mother to visit an old lady named Lida, who lived alone. She was a very old woman, I thought then—probably at least 50—and a little scary to me because she had wild white hair, and she would embrace me so thoroughly that I couldn't breathe. We went often to see her—not my favorite thing—and always brought food. I had never known who Lida was until the other day, when I asked my sister, Eileen. It turns out that one day my mother received a phone call from a wrong number. On the other end of the line was a lonely old lady. My mother was her friend until Lida's death a few years later. In my memory, this was the first in a long line of strays and lonely people that she took in as her responsibility.

One day a few years ago we were in the grocery store together, and a strange woman stopped us in the aisle. It was a lengthy, animated conversation. She was telling my mother about her children and her house and her business, and I only half-listened. As she was about to leave, she put her hand on my arm. "Your mom changed my life," she said. "I was going through a rough time, and she gave our family Christmas. It was the one thing I needed to know that I wasn't alone. Ever since, I have tried to do the same thing for other people, and I have taught my children to do it, too."

My mother was so proud of that. She never had any recognition for the things she did, and I doubt she thought she deserved any. But she was the kind of person who just did things because they needed doing. When her own mother died, Ethel was just 18, and had a 12-year-old brother. She was working full-time, but she kept house for her father and raised her baby brother.

These last years without my father, and then without her beloved dog, were difficult and lonely, but they were lived exactly as she chose. She was, as she liked to say, the Captain of her own ship, and she never gave up her command.

As we say goodbye to her today, we salute her warmth, her generosity, her love, and even her temper. She was her own person to the end. And that is her legacy.

26

GATHERING STORM

My mother died ten days ago, and I haven't cried. What I mean to say is that I have shed some tears, but I haven't wept. I know that grief has its own path, but it feels wrong that I have been so business-like and dry-eyed. For reasons of my own, I am re-reading *The Odyssey*, and in Homeric literature there is an understanding that weeping and tears are essential tributes to the dead. Not crying is wrong.

People tell me that she was a great age, and it is natural. That is true. But age does not make death any more welcome. Someone reminded me yesterday of a happy event a few months past, and my heart went straight to the distinction between now and then: My mother is gone now. Then, she was on this earth, only a phone call or a drive away. Now she is gone forever, unreachable, untouchable, all hurts and old wounds now frozen into permanent scars, all love and tenderness irrelevant.

Our priest asked us at the cemetery whether we wanted to stay to watch her lowered into the earth, and to the dismay of my sister, I said yes, and everyone else felt compelled to stay at my wish. We tucked her in next to my father, the hard edge of his vault visible after six years, a blanket of orange and magenta roses waiting to be laid across her grave.

My tribute, I suppose, is still unpaid. I think it will burst upon me like a sudden storm, splattering innocent passersby whether they are sympathetic or not.

And that is the way of grief.

27

LOVE AND GRIEF

My husband likes to say that Moses is a tuning fork. He is our German Shepherd who loves by pure concentration. His every focus is on those he loves, and he trembles when he senses our stress. The night I left to go to my mother in her last crisis, he fought to be with me where he could not come, even as Charlie lovingly urged him to stay at home. In his distress, gentle Moses put his teeth on Charlie for trying to stop him from getting in my car. It was a protest, not an attack. But my leaving Moses behind was a betrayal to us both.

As a comfort and a way of drawing out my stillborn sorrow, I have been re-reading Madeleine L'Engle's adolescent novels, which are explorations of faith and mortality. I keep hoping they will provoke my grief eventually, if not immediately. My own faith, so relatively new and untested, is approximately the same as the novel series' teenager as she encounters death for the first time: in a friend's father, in a friend's illness, then in her grandfather. At the same time in the story, a dolphin's baby dies, and the teenage protagonist writes a poem. Maybe it isn't great poetry, but I like it because it expresses the value of life and love regardless of the boundaries of species. In it, the angels weep because every life matters even in the span of the universe.

I am in a place where I am gathering all the love I can find. And the love of Moses, who sleeps now at my feet, is a treasure as deep as any I can claim.

The devotion of dogs is not new. Homer acknowledges the love of Argos, the dog of Odysseus, who, waiting twenty years for the return of his master, is neglected, flea-ridden, and sleeping on a pile of dung. And yet, when Argos at last sees his master—even though no human creature recognizes him—Argos wags his tail in greeting to the one he has always loved and dies. Odysseus, who has endured the battle of Troy, Sirens, Circe, the Cyclops, Scylla and Charybdis, the deaths of all his companions, and the wrath of Poseidon, nevertheless weeps for the love of his old dog.

Moses is a dog. And his deep love for me is as real and palpable as any other love I know. He grieves when I grieve, and he is filled with joy when I am. What is love, if not this? And what greater comfort in grief than this deep devotion?

His soul reaches out to me, and, gratefully, I answer.

28

THE GOING PRICE FOR SQUIRRELS

My sister from out of town is staying at our lake cottage. She is being respectful of my writing time while she works on our late mother's house, doing many things that I am tired of doing. She told me she didn't want to distract me, and that I shouldn't be worrying about her during this period of intense writing. But she did want to borrow a dog for company. Well, not "a" dog. She wanted snuggly, sweet Pete.

On her first night there, she announced that we had mice or something in the ceiling. I did not find this alarming. Mice kind of come along with cottages, and as much as I love animals, having seen what they do when we're away, even I have been forced to take a hard line. So, the situation did not seem particularly alarming or challenging. But when my sister began to describe what she was experiencing, it began to seem unlikely that mice were the culprits. Scampering, twittering, scrabbling, and, yes, chewing.

I am living my own novel.

We went out to the cottage that night and were sitting on the couch drinking wine, looking at family treasures my sister had unearthed, when she stopped me and said: listen.

Above our heads, we heard what I can only describe as the kind of squeals and squeaking you expect to hear in a Disney animation. This was not a squirrel. This was a colony. At least. And it had happened so fast. We hadn't been away for more than two weeks. It was alarming. There were many, many, many animals up there. And they were apparently rather busy. From the sound of things, they were singing to themselves as they made a dress for the ball.

My husband gave me the lecture: you cannot be soft-hearted about this. You must call an exterminator. There is no other way. I nodded and pretended to look reasonable, but I confess that I had no intention of exterminating an entire neighborhood of baby squirrels. Sometimes, I wonder if he knows me at all.

The next day, I called a company that my friend had once used to remove a bat. Or a raccoon. Or both. They specialize in trapping and releasing wild animals that have taken up residence in your house. They assured me that they would not harm the squirrels, and that they even had a squirrel expert—although he had injured his back and was not as available as usual. They charge $149 for the house call, and $39 per squirrel.

They will be there at eight-thirty this morning. And I suspect that the bill will be rather high.

29

AND THE EARTH STANDS STILL

I found myself in the position, recently, of explaining Holy Week to someone who does not believe. Perhaps a bit too earnestly, I tried to describe what happens: the triumph of Palm Sunday with its awful portent, the congregation taking the part of Christ's accusers, facing—whether we want to or not—our own sins; the washing of the feet, and the ritual vigil, kept with Christ throughout the night on Maundy Thursday; on Friday, the awful full-eyed clarity of the torture and agony of the crucifixion and then, at last, the breath of life gone, the Pascal candle extinguished, the altar stripped, and the deep internal stillness of grief hanging over the congregants.

We are all diminished by every death. But this one death is ours and His. The fear of it lingers in our hearts as we wait in hope.

It is Good Friday. And the earth stands still.

30

MOVING TOWARD THE SUN

I love winter. This past week of snow and bitter cold delighted and invigorated me. I can't quite explain why. Maybe it has something to do with the light and the transformation of the world into a different place.

But getting up in the dark is very, very hard. This morning, as I awoke, the great horned owls were still singing to one another deep in the woods, and the dogs startled the deer who like to browse in the darkness.

Today, however, even though the sunrise will keep getting later and later, the hours of light begin to lengthen. In deepest winter, we find ourselves thinking about the path we are beginning towards the longest day in summer. In summer, the joy of that long day is tinged with sadness that the days will begin to shorten. Now, the darkness is enlivened by the hope of spring.

Two of our friends have lost parents this week. They are deeply religious people, so I imagine their grief is filled with this same mixture of despair and promise: the paradox of faith. As they gaze out on this new and alien landscape of their lives, may they find the consolation of light and hope.

31

NOW ME ALSO COMMENTING HERE

When writers get together, the conversation immediately moves to the vicissitudes of publishing: which house treats authors well; who never issues checks on time; what kind of publicity is offered. And in these days of social media madness, the subject of blogging is always high on the list of topics.

If you're a writer, you have to have a blog. And if you have a blog, you live for comments. But you are always lured into disappointment by spam. "You have 162 comments!" your blog site tells you. Eagerly, you check in, only to discover that your comments are 100 percent spam.

Maybe I'm missing something, but I don't understand how spam works. Most of the come-on attempts are so patently false, and—at least on my blogging system—so completely separated out from the genuine, that I almost feel sorry for the perpetrators. Almost.

Remember Mad Libs? It's a party game in which you are instructed to come up with a list of words: a noun, a verb, another noun, an adjective. And then your words are inserted into a previously unknown paragraph, with hilarious results.

Spam comments always remind me of this. And this is why I am puzzled.

Somewhere in the world, someone has provided a list of English synonyms to be inserted into standard sentences for the express purpose of permitting miscreants to invade your website and computer. Maybe the mastermind behind it played Mad Libs games as a child. Or maybe he has an unwarranted confidence in the intellect of his minions. And not incidentally, he may be underestimating the intelligence of the average blog writer.

To wit:

(All errors below are as written by senders.)

"I've been browsing online more than 3 hours today, yet I never found any interesting article like yours. It is pretty worth enough for me."

"Personally if all web owners and blogrrss made good content as youu did, the net will be much more useful than ever before."

"i've read this put up and iff I maay desire to suggest soke fascinating issues of suggestions."

"Ahaa, its good conversation not he topic of this article here at this website, I have read all that, so now me also commenting here."

"Thank you for the auspicious writeup. It in fact was a amusement account it. Look advanced to more added agreeable from you!"

One fellow (non-spam) writer confessed to me that she was so fearful of contamination from these comments that she was afraid even to look at them. She was missing the opportunity for some fine comedy.

But all the same, I am deeply grateful for spam filters. And I look advanced to your comments.

32

THE IMPLAUSIBILITY OF TURKEYS

It is dusk. That blue time between light and shadow when the winter night begins to close. There is a fire in the fireplace, the red-shaded lamps are lit, and the candles, which have burned all afternoon to scent the room, are dwindling into embers. The dogs, restless from insufficient exercise, are at last asleep, one on his bed near the fire, the other in a cooler spot on the rug near the front door.

The windows are not yet dark, and in the tops of the trees, the turkeys are beginning to fly up to their roosts. Ungainly, ugly things, who look as if flight should be impossible, one by one, they startle up and nestle into the very tops of the wind-blown trees. It starts with one. Then a pause. Then one and two, and then, in some sequence of whim or order, the flock rises into its berths. The exact location changes every night.

How they manage to stay in place all night is difficult to imagine. It seems wrong that such enormous birds should perch on such delicate branches, sometimes fanning out their feathers so that, from a distance, they appear like giant balls attached to the top of a tree.

At dawn, they will repeat the same event in reverse, until, with the climbing sun, they pick their way in a ramshackle line from the woods, through the orchard, and across the street to the neighbor's yard.

Their track is hard-packed and wide through the snow.

33

SLOW TURNING

I was up before dark this morning, as I am almost every morning. But today, I was caught by the beginning light, and I stopped to watch the sunrise.

I kept checking to see if I was mistaken, but it became increasingly clear how far north the sun has moved. Or, more correctly, how much we have moved toward the sun. Every day this week, the sun rises one minute earlier and sets one minute later. By now, it's enough extra light to mean the dogs get a run in our favorite woods rather than a mundane walk.

I have dogs to feed, reports to read and meetings to attend, and an unfinished novel. My days are mostly the same.

Still, the cosmos moves in its slow turning toward spring.

Meanwhile, there's still time for a blizzard. It's what I want for my birthday.

34

FIRST SING

When we were newly married, my husband and I had an agreement. Whenever I said I "hated" something, I owed him a dollar; whenever he interrupted me, he owed me a dollar. I hated bad grammar. I hated vinyl siding. I hated... you know...unimportant things. He still interrupts me incessantly. But, I rarely say that I hate anything. I'm good with that. Not with the interrupting, really, but marriage is about compromise. I mean, it's better not to express so much negativity about trivialities.

So, you will, perhaps, appreciate the intensity and genuine feeling expressed when I tell you that I hate daylight savings time. Much of that is about being an early riser. After months of the dreariness of rising in pitch black and turning on the lights as if you'd never gone to bed, we had finally been waking in the faint light of pre-dawn. It was easier, and life had a rhythm to it. Even on days off, my body clock would chime, and I would rise at the usual time. It made the mornings effortless.

But last night, we couldn't get to sleep because it was

too early, and this morning, after a restless night with odd and vivid dreams, getting up was dark, and hard, and miserable. It was jet lag—but imposed without the lovely trip to London.

I dragged myself to the kitchen for coffee and returned to the bedroom to sit by the window and watch the stirrings of life in the woods. The room felt overheated, so I threw open a window. What I heard made me stand up and go to the doors and open them to listen, just to be sure. Mixed with the turkeys, and the geese on the lake, and the red squirrels, was the song of the first robins. Flocks of them, not just one.

March is early for robins in Wisconsin. Maybe this warm weather is more than just a tease.

35

AN EDITING CAUTIONARY TALE

We are in the final edits—the galleys—of *North of the Tension Line* just at the very moment that things are intense at work. Although a professional proofreader and my editor have been through the book, as the author, I, too, need to review it, and time is pretty crunched. My good friend, Mary Beth, aka "Impromptu Librarian," offered to be an extra set of eyes, and I gratefully accepted. In less than a day, she had read the book for probably the third time, and returned the proofed documents for me to pass on to my editor. But the next morning, she called, and we had an odd conversation.

Mary Beth: "What is hapcedarss?"

Me: "I'm sorry?"

Mary Beth: "Hapcedarss."

Me: "I hate your bluetooth system."

Mary Beth: "It's in your book. Hapcedarss."

Me: "Hapcedarss? It's in my book? Are you sure?"

Mary Beth: "I'm sure. The proofreader has many notes about it."

Me: "In *my* book?"

Mary Beth: "She had been commenting on it several times, and then pointed out that she had googled the word and checked with OED but cannot find any such word."

Me: "That's hardly surprising. I don't think there is any such word."

Mary Beth: "Well, it's in your book."

Me: "Hapcedarss is in my book."

Mary Beth: "Right."

Me: "Hmmm. Very odd."

It was a busy day of meetings and preparations for meetings at work, so it wasn't until quite late that, now having forgotten about hapcedarss, I was finally able to sit down with my manuscript to begin my own proofreading. Not far into the manuscript, light finally dawned.

I sold my book much more quickly than I had expected, so submitting my manuscript for fact-checking had therefore also had a much tighter timeline than I had expected. Among the more essential things was sending the book to my friend Captain Bill, the ferry captain, to make sure that I hadn't committed any egregious ferrying errors. He called me, and in one of the more delightful moments of this whole process, left a message telling me that he had read the book, and that he had liked it. I still have his voicemail on my phone and listen to it when I'm feeling blue. Anyway, when I called him back, I anxiously enquired whether I had made any mistakes about the ferry or said anything stupid about the lake or its navigation. He assured me that it was all fine, but he had one correction. The trees at School House Beach, he pointed out, were not pines, as I had written. They were cedars.

Armed with this information, I sat down with my manuscript and created a "find and replace." Wherever P-I-N-E appeared, it should be replaced with C-E-D-A-R. For some reason, I have rarely used find and replace, even though I have been using this software at home and at work for a pretty long time. What I hadn't realized was that find and replace doesn't just find and replace words. It finds and replaces the interiors of words.

It was late in the day, but I called my editor in New York. "I'm so glad you called to tell me this," she said. "I had a terrible day, and this makes it so much better."

Apparently, there is a great deal of happiness—or at least the talk of it—in my book. And it's likely that hapcedarss will forever be a part of Mary Beth's, and my, and my editor's vocabularies.

Our cups overflow with hapcedarss.

36

THE BEST THINGS HAPPEN WHEN YOU AREN'T LOOKING

We have some major landscaping going on here, and the place looks like a moonscape. There have been bulldozers and skid steers, the power company (three times), the stone and gravel guy, and, of course, a perfectly-timed autumn deluge to delay the whole process and increase the pleasure of muddy dogs and white bedspreads. No distractions here.

We live in the woods, and if there's one thing we have a great deal of, it's firewood. We had promised our neighbor and stalwart friend, Mark, that he could have the rather enormous stack down in the woods. It's long and difficult to drag that wood up the hill by hand, and he had been slowly tackling it over the course of the past year. With the new grading, though, it was suddenly possible to get his pickup down there without damaging anything, so we were hurrying—in advance of the deluge—to load up the wood in the truck while we still could. We were down in the woods, throwing logs into the truck, unaware of what was going on up at the house.

When I came in to clean up for dinner, there was a UPS

delivery by the side door: a big stack of boxes. I swear, it took me nearly three minutes to realize what they were: 100 copies of my first book, *North of the Tension Line.*

All of my life in this one moment.

37

ONE DAY IN SPRING

We live in an old house in a neighborhood that was once part of an orchard. Like our neighbors, we have remnants of the orchard on our property, along with a magnificent collection of very large crab apple trees. The trees are old enough to be inconvenient. They haven't been genetically modified to produce tiny hard apples or fruit that doesn't fall. They make a mess, and they attract wasps. But unlike the modern varieties, they have a larger purpose in life than mere looks: they bear big, delicious fruit. The apples are a nuisance to pick, and I rarely have time to harvest them. We have more than one variety, but one tree in particular has fruit whose flavor explodes in your mouth, tart and fragrant. It's an experience to remember in old age, like the smell of fall leaves when you are lying underneath them in a big pile; the odd feeling of emerging from the airport in the early morning on your first trip to Europe; or one kiss on one night.

The tree by our house is the largest crab apple I've ever seen. It must be close to eighty years old, and it is so tall that it hangs over the roof. During our recent construction, the builders and the landscape people wanted to cut it down. It's too close to the house. They told me it wouldn't live much longer, and I might as well do it now while everything was dug up. The roots would get in the way of the foundation. The cedar shakes on the roof needed less shade. They almost convinced me. I'm allergic to wasps, and I don't have time to deal with high maintenance anything.

But in the end, I couldn't do it. We made our kitchen smaller.

Every year, we watch with anticipation for the moment when the trees all come into bloom. And most years, we are disappointed. I can remember only one year when we were able to fully enjoy the trees in sunshine and birdsong for their entire bloom. Usually, it rains and the rain washes all the blossoms away before we've had a chance to enjoy them. We joke about getting only three days a year.

I have been watching the weather earnestly this past week or so, because the blossoms are about to pop. They are so much more glorious in the sunshine. We had snowflakes here yesterday and frost last night. I had a fire in the fireplace while I waited for my husband to return from Washington. The forecast is rain and clouds all next week.

But today is the day. The sun rose in full glory with not one single cloud, and the trees are miraculously blooming. Everything sparkles, and the colors of early spring are young and rich. I can't tell yet whether the frost did any damage, but the window of my little study is filled with the rosy blossoms of the grand tree. Today may be all we get, but it is worth the trouble.

In the end, I suppose, I'm not a very practical person. But we get this one day in spring.

38

ANOTHER SIGN OF SPRING

For some reason, my husband decided yesterday to take Moses to the barber shop with him.

Don't ask.

One factor may have been that the night before, Moses had had a rather thorough bath, complete with shampoo and conditioner, as opposed to the daily rinse in the dog shower he usually gets to clean his feet. He was smelling good and was all soft and shiny, and this seemed like an opportunity to give him a good brushing. Thought for the day: never brush a wet dog. Especially not in the house. No, not even if it's really cold and miserable outside.

German Shepherds are a breed that have a spring molt, which is referred to as "blowing their coats." An odd expression, I thought, in my innocence. But that was before. Now that he is four and officially fully mature, Moses is having his first real blowing-of-the-coat, and I have come to think that whoever coined the phrase had a gift for understatement. Moses's long black hair with its creamy roots is coming out in massive tufts, which do indeed blow. Everywhere. Piling up in insane quantities in the corner behind the kitchen door. Stuck to the stamp on the Easter card I sent to my aunt. Appearing, unexpectedly—and disturbingly—in my coffee cup at work. But this was nothing compared to the wet dog hair that he and I, together, artfully distributed about the mud room, on the white kitchen cabinets, and on my person. There is no broom, no vacuum, no lint roller sufficient to the task. It's like glue, and your only hope is to wait for it to dry and then wipe it off with a dry rag.

NASA ought to look into potential applications.

In any case, and for whatever reason, Moses had a trip to the barber shop. He was permitted to wander around and sniff at things, he obligingly lay on his back to have his tummy rubbed by several admirers, and when asked, he lay quietly on the floor nearby while my husband had his hair cut, all amidst the chaos of dryers, and razors, and customers coming and going. He was, in short, a very good dog.

It would have been nice if a trip to the barber shop had resulted in a bit less dog hair, but I suppose I should just be grateful that he was shedding somewhere else for a while.

39

A WOMAN OF A CERTAIN AGE

I noticed Christie Brinkley on the cover of a magazine at the grocery store recently. She is in her sixties, apparently, and looking as beautiful as ever. She was already grown up when I was a child, but she still looks better than I do, even with her head start in years. This point was driven home to me rather hard recently.

My husband had a big event. It was black tie. And remembering—as one does—only that I once looked nice in evening wear, I did not feel any sense of impending alarm. It would be simple, I thought, to find something lovely—not too youthful but elegant and simple, mind you—that I could wear. I imagined not that people would gasp when I entered the room, but merely that they would notice that I was respectable.

And maybe pretty for a woman of a certain age.

I began with a sense of calm. I had plenty of time. I even imagined that I might lose a pound or two. But as time went on, and I still had not managed to eliminate wine, or bread, or cheese from my diet, I realized that I needed to work with what I had.

I should point out—since it's necessary for this story—that I used to be an opera singer. I once had a closet full of beautiful gowns, many of them custom made to my design. My brother used to tease me that I had become a singer just for the wardrobe, and he may have been right.

There was a black taffeta strapless gown with a bow on the bodice and a little gold-trimmed red velvet jacket that could be worn over it for maximum versatility when I was traveling and giving more than one concert. There was a plum velvet gown with long sleeves and an off-the-shoulder neckline. For recitals, there was a white one that I had copied from a Sargent painting, with a long pink and periwinkle blue sashes. There was a burgundy damask with a train that I wore with matching suede Louis XIV heels. There was an ivory one with a sheer metallic gold overlay. And there was the black one with long sleeves, a slit up the front that showed leg when I walked, and a sweep on either side, rather like Morticia Adams. I wore it when I sang *Carmina Burana*. It was so low-cut that a friend told me later she said a prayer every time I leaned over to take a drink of water during the concert.

As a result of having had this lovely wardrobe, I came to be a trifle bored by the strapless, big-skirted ball gown that was cutting edge then, but is utterly commonplace now. I was not interested in anything like that for this grown-up event.

With my singing days far behind me, I soon discovered

that my task would not be easy. I found mostly mother-of-the-bride kinds of things, and even though I am definitely middle-aged, I don't think of myself as a matron. Not what I was hoping for. I tried on other things that seemed like they might be okay. But they were too tight. Or too revealing. Or too…something. The phrase of a British friend echoed repeatedly in my mind: "mutton dressed as lamb." Surely, there must be something suitable for a woman of a certain age who still wanted to look elegant? Not trying too hard?

So, at last, feeling frustrated and at the increasingly insistent urging of the sales clerk, I agreed to try the respectable but boring, strapless, full-skirted ball gown in emerald green satin. It was beautiful, and beautifully made, and very expensive. At this point, I didn't care how much it was. I had to find something. Innocently, I assumed that the style would still flatter. Strapless gowns have always been my fall-back position. In the dressing room, I put on the borrowed heels and the full petticoat that were provided by the shop and headed out to the mirror.

It's funny how your perception of yourself stays back at the age of thirty, and the rest of you descends from there. I knew I had gained weight, but I had been under the illusion that I was still okay. And maybe in my office uniform of dark suit and heels, that illusion can be maintained. But in a strapless gown, not so much. I was so…puffy…so plump. My arms were full and any muscles were rendered invisible by a layer of insulation. My eyes looked small and tired, and the expression on my face was grim. There was a resemblance, though, that hung along the edges of my awareness that I couldn't quite place. I looked familiar, but not like myself.

The saleswoman fussed around me, saying how elegant it was, how suitable, but I kept trying to grasp the elusive idea that flitted like an errant swallow in my brain. I stood in the lights, staring at the image in the mirror. And then suddenly, the thought settled, and it hit me: Oh my God. I look like Mary Todd Lincoln.

I was back in the dressing room, pulling off the gown and putting on my own clothes as quickly as I could, desperate to get out of there.

The sales lady professed not to understand, but that's her job—to tell you that you look beautiful. That the dress suits you. She's not going to admit that you do, in fact, resemble a nineteenth-century dowager at an inaugural ball. Poor Mary. So dumpy. So dour. So misunderstood. So unhappy.

I left the shop as quickly as possible and went home to cruise the internet for something black and shapeless. As far as I know, no one has yet invented formal sweat pants. I think there would be a market.

40

GOING WITH THE FLOW

My niece's wedding took place on a dock on Baltimore's Inner Harbor, a fashionably updated working harbor surrounded by sailing ships, industrial areas, refurbished warehouses, and chic shops and restaurants. It was a formal wedding, with the bride in cream satin, five bridesmaids in teal organza, and the groom and groomsmen in classic black tuxedoes.

Among the various tourist attractions on the Harbor is a pirate ship. It has lots of flags and sails, and a skull-and-crossbones, and its purpose, apparently, is for people to get happily sloshed while sailing around and experiencing various kinds of pirate schtick, all electronically amplified. It's not clear to me exactly what this involves. Maybe, it's something like the routines flight attendants on Southwest Airlines used to do, only with a swashbuckling theme, and probably a cannon or something. Anyway, the bride had been warned by the venue that the ship made regular trips on Saturday afternoons, and that the pirates and their passengers tended to be somewhat…uninhibited.

Sure enough, just after the officiant had begun the service and The Sainted Aunt had been invited to come forward to speak, the pirate ship made its appearance, accompanied by amplified uproar. Naturally, it was impossible to speak over this, so the ceremony paused, and everyone turned to watch the ship go by. This took some time. Everyone on the pirate ship waved, and the entire bridal party and guests all waved back. A ceremonial ARRRRRRRRRR was raised from the ship, and the guests responded in kind.

No matter what else was said and done that day after more than a year of planning—what the vows were, what music was played, what was on the menu at the reception—I'm pretty sure that this act of exuberant spontaneity,and the response to it, is the one thing everyone will remember twenty years from now.

Another lesson for married life.

41

LETTER TO A POET

We have never met, but our lives have passed very near to one another, and you have unknowingly changed my life.

When I was seven years old, my piano teacher was Reuel Kenyon. I went to Newport Elementary School down the street from his house in Ann Arbor, but he came to our house to give me lessons. I don't know that I was a particularly good student, but I did eventually become a professional musician—an opera singer—and I remember him fondly. I also remember him telling my mother that his daughter, Jane, was getting married to a university professor. I studied with him for three years before my family moved away.

At the same time, my older brother was one of your students at the University of Michigan. I was a very little girl, but he came home and read to me the poetry he was studying in your classes. He taught me about the ancient stopped rhythms in "Baa, Baa, Black Sheep," and "Hark! Hark! The Dogs Do Bark!" He read many things to me from class, but he most particularly loved Theodore Roethke. He bought a Caedmon recording of the poet reading his works, and we would listen to it again and again until we both knew all the poems by heart. To this day, those words are embedded on my heart and brain, and I feel that they belong particularly to me.

Eventually, I acquired other recordings of poets reading their work, and the power and value of memorizing their poetry makes it baffling to me that memorization is so sneered at by modern teachers. These things in my life have been a tremendous gift.

I have read and enjoyed your books, and I delight in your poetry and that of your late wife. I read, with sorrow, your account of her death and wept with you and for you both.

So, today, perhaps by coincidence, after tucking one of your books into a shelf in my office, I went online and happened upon the essay, "Between Solitude and Loneliness." I had read the first few paragraphs before I suddenly saw your byline, and something compelled me to write. That line between the two states is one I have difficulty navigating, and even though I am a woman in my fifties, I'm still not completely certain I have formulated the right recipe for myself.

I am sitting at my desk in the bright sunshine of a late winter afternoon in Wisconsin, procrastinating over my writing. A dog-eared copy of Theodore Roethke's *On Poetry & Craft* sits within reach, along with *So, You Want to Own an Oil Tanker* (I don't); *Your Goats* (I have none); and Cicero's *On A Life Well Spent* (I do struggle with procrastination). Their commonality is that they are research for my next novel.

I don't know whether it will mean anything to you, but I wanted to tell you that even though you were never actually my teacher, your passion for words profoundly influenced me and my life, and for that I am genuinely grateful.

They are probably not to your taste, but I am sending you copies of my two novels, which are part of a series. In the first one, the poetry-writing ferry captain has an experience that is very loosely based on Roethke's account of the inspiration for "Four for Sir John Davies." In both, the main character struggles with her loneliness and manages, mostly, to ride it out to someplace happier. Perhaps they will entertain you a little.

I wish you good health, a good view, and the luxury of solitude unblemished by loneliness.

42

CROSSROADS

It is a jittery place, knowing that your book is out there and that strangers are reading it. *North of the Tension Line* is off press and ready to ship, so any errors in editing are now permanent. But the hundreds of Advance Reading Copies are out there like little seeds, taking root or dying. There are so many things to worry about, but they are all things that are stupid to worry about, because they are beyond my control. I can't make people like the book. I can't re-read anymore and correct. I can only wait and hope. And try not to wait and hope.

As any writer knows, you put your heart out there and hope that no one stomps it.

It will be a good night for a long romp with the dogs. And possibly a cocktail.

43

NOT JUDGING BOOKS BY THEIR COVERS

I had car trouble recently on my way to a signing in Door County. I was tooling along at 70 mph in the pouring rain, when all of a sudden, there was some catastrophic electronic failure. Every dire warning sign flicked on the dashboard. I lost my brakes, I lost my power steering, and the engine began to buck. Fortunately, I was close to an exit in civilization, which for our purposes here means a place with a Mazda dealer only a few miles away, and was able to coast and manhandle the car down a ramp, through a roundabout, and into the parking lot of a minimart.

I hate roundabouts. I mean, I hated them before, but in this case, it was lucky I didn't have to stop. I could just keep coasting.

When I pulled up next to the building out of the way, all the lights in the dashboard went out, and I couldn't turn off the engine. I had to go inside to figure out where I was, so I could tell the tow truck where to come. Normally, one doesn't leave a running car unattended. *But what the hell,* I thought. *It's not as if anyone could drive it away.*

None of this is the point of the story, but I kind of wanted to tell it.

The tow truck showed up in about ten minutes to my surprise and relief. I was cutting it a little close to get to my event on time, and I was having a hard time figuring out how to explain to the bookstore proprietor—my friend, Peter—that all his planning may be for an authorless book signing. I called my husband, who was speeding in my direction to rescue me, and told him he could go back.

Anyway—and now we're getting to the nub of the thing—the tow truck driver was this young, blond guy with lots of tattoos. He was a kind of classic Wisconsin small-town guy, complete with the rural accent: decent, trustworthy, competent, grease on his clothes, dirt under his nails. He hooked up my car, and I climbed into the cab of the truck for the ride to the (mercifully) open car dealer, who would loan me a car.

I told him that I was in a bit of a hurry, because there was an event I had to be at. What kind of event, he wanted to know? So, I told him I was a writer.

"I love books!" he said. "Harry Potter is my favorite, as you can probably tell by these." He raised his left arm to indicate his tattoos, which I couldn't really see, but which must have been representative of this passion. "I listen mostly to audio books, though." He fumbled in his pocket to get out his iPhone while I hoped that he was looking at the highway. "I've listened to..." he looked down at his phone to check the exact figure "...two months and two-and-a-half weeks worth of books this year so far." He then proceeded to talk about his favorites. After Harry Potter, there was a series of World War I historical novels by Ken Follett and some other series in a similar vein. He was knowledgeable about history, and he clearly loved stories of heroism and mysticism. He wanted to know if my books were on audio. I told him not yet, but that we were working on it.

"I read paper books, too," he said. "But with all the driving around, I do mostly audio." I kind of doubt that my books are his kind of thing, but so far, all my assumptions were being proved false. "Would you like a copy of my book?" I asked. He was enthusiastic.

We got to the dealer, and I dug out a copy of each of my books and signed them for him. We shook hands.

I love thinking about this tow truck driver, wandering around the country roads of Wisconsin, doing this necessary but unglamorous job, the rhythms of different authorial voices accompanying his travels, moved by the heroic acts of protagonists both real and imagined. Along what path will these experiences take him? How will these stories affect his life and the lives of others? From the seemingly mundane heroism of helping people with broken cars to some other, more dramatic form? Or is it these small daily rescues that give his path meaning?

Maybe he thinks about these things. Or maybe not. Maybe it's just a job to him, not a mission. But the meanings of our lives may be things we never realize until we're looking back. Or they could be things we'll never know.

People are always more interesting than you think.

44

THE KINDNESS OF STRANGERS

In the interest of realism—as opposed to self-pity—it is reasonable to point out that the life of an unknown author on a book tour is not glamorous. It is, in fact, lonely, discouraging, and humbling in the truest sense of the word. You know how people win the Nobel Prize and say it is humbling? Well, winning the Nobel Prize is not humbling. No. Waking up alone in a hotel room, driving all day, having a book event where four people show up in a room set up for 35, and then going alone to another hotel room —*that* is humbling.

I am not complaining. At least not at this moment. This is all part of the process of breaking into a difficult business as an unknown author. If I persist, I hope someday I can increase my audience turnout to something more respectable. Possibly even to double it. I am merely pointing out how meaningful interactions with people can be in these circumstances. The other night in Lake Orion, Michigan, after a day of this kind, I decided to take myself out for a nice dinner. And possibly a cocktail. Possibly more than one.

It was a Saturday night. The place was packed, and the

wait for a table was over an hour. So, I found a single place at the bar, an advantage to traveling alone, and decided to have my dinner there. There was a couple seated next to me—I was on the corner—and we started chatting. We talked for well over an hour. They were parents whose first child was a freshman in college, and they were struggling with parenting withdrawal, and I was deeply grateful for the conversation. They generously asked questions about my book. I gave them a book card and wished that I had a book with me to give to them. When they left, we all exchanged good wishes, but I didn't realize until I was ready to leave a little while later that they had paid my bill. I didn't have a chance to thank them.

So, to the couple at the bar in Lake Orion please accept my thanks. Your gesture was gratefully received and will be duly passed along to someone else who may appreciate it.

Cheers.

45

BETWEEN DESPAIR AND PRIDE

I am reading some essays by Wendell Berry in which he captures with great simplicity and concision the necessity of loneliness. I think that is one of the reasons I love Washington Island so much. When I say that I feel more myself there than anywhere else, I think it is because I am alone there and lonely there.

Loneliness is frightening. And that is part of what is necessary, but I mitigate my loneliness with my dogs. They are soulful and joyous companions, and I need them, because the intensity of my emotion is sometimes threatening.

I would never walk in the woods in the dark without them, even though Moses likes to pretend he is a wolf, running off to return and stalk me silently along the far edges of the path. This is his great game, and he makes me feel that I am in a Russian fairy tale.

But in this loneliness, there is also a settling in to the essence of self. It's not an exercise in ego, but an escape from it. It feels, as the nonessential is pulled away, that the course of life is running along its proper path. I am simply myself. Again, and for the first time. Theodore Roethke wrote, "What falls away is always, and is near." I think this experience is what he was referring to.

All this is to say that it has been a long time since I have been to the Island for any length of time, and I need to go there. My trip was almost cancelled this week by other kinds of necessity, and the thought of not being able to go created a rising panic that started deep. I need to go there to let the world fall away. I need myself back.

Berry talks of the right place in life as being between despair and pride. They are his opposites. That is what I need—to be in the right place.

46

HEIGH-HO! THE GLAMOROUS LIFE

So many writers have written about the humiliation of book tours, the awkwardness of sitting at a table waiting for strangers to approach. There are people who don't want to buy a book and feel that it would be a form of rejection to stop and not purchase one (and they're right), but I hadn't realized how many people are simply just shy. I watched today as people carefully turned their heads so as not to have to see me sitting alone at the table at Barnes & Noble. For the people who didn't care, it was easy. I could hail them and offer a bookmark, which they could take or not, and they could then wander on. But there were several people whom I knew perfectly well wanted to engage in conversation, but who couldn't bring themselves to do it. They lingered agonizingly near, sometimes for nearly an hour, but could never position themselves in such a way that I could catch their glance or smile and thus invite conversation.

I knew them, because they were me. I remember sitting next to Beverly Sills at dinner for an entire evening and hardly knowing what to say to her. I was 18 years old and wanted so much to be an opera singer just like her, but I couldn't think of a single thing to say. Ultimately, she took pity on me, but it was an opportunity missed.

Today, I am going to see if I can engage more people. If nothing else, it will be a way to pass the time.

47

INTRODUCTION OF CHARLES KRAUTHAMMER

In this age of tweeted selfies, twerking and Miley Cyrus, Charles Krauthammer is that rare and essential thing: a public intellectual.

He is, by most estimates, the nation's leading conservative commentator, noted for his insight, his wit, and his clarity of mind.

An alumnus of McGill, Balliol, and Harvard, trained as a doctor, along the way he re-invented himself as a writer. He has described his life story as improbable and characterized by serendipity and sheer blind luck.

He is the originator of the phrase "The Reagan Doctrine," and he has been a keen observer of, and indeed, a profound influence on American foreign policy for over three decades.

He is distinguished by being, in his own words, "the only entity on earth, other than rogue states, that has received an apology from the White House."

And he is a fierce opponent of the errant comma.

His most recent book, *Things That Matter: Three Decades of Passions, Pastimes and Politics*, is a collection of his columns. It is a wide-ranging demonstration of the breadth of his interests and the fluency of his thinking, all built on the fundamental premise that politics is just a means to an end; That it exists only to make possible the things that matter: friendship, love, art, philosophy, baseball, science, chess, nature. Politics, for all its banality, is the essential platform for these real things. And if politics goes wrong, all these things—the things that matter—are destroyed.

In reading Dr. Krauthammer's book you will learn—if you hadn't already known it—that he is a man of deep feeling. The ringing simplicity of his eulogies to his brother, his mentor, his friend, the subtlety of his humor, and his relish for the ridiculous make his writings both companionable and engrossing.

And if the underlying compassion of his essays is not evidence enough of his character, Dr. Krauthammer is a dog lover. At the passing of his son's black lab, Chester, he wrote:

> Some will protest that in a world with so much human suffering, it is something between eccentric and obscene to mourn a dog. I think not. After all, it is perfectly normal, indeed deeply human to be moved when nature presents us with a vision of great beauty.
>
> Should we not be moved when it produces a vision—a creature—of the purest sweetness?

And should we here tonight not be privileged to encounter a man of such depth and fundamental humanity?

—March 6, 2014, Centennial Hall, Milwaukee, Wisconsin

48

LETTER TO ROSE

Thank you for your lovely notes. You cannot know how much they touch my heart. Our summer has not been the best, as you might imagine. Cleaning out Mom's house has been a dreadful and melancholy chore (not yet completed), which, thank God, Eileen has been here to supervise. Although she did much of the work alone while I was at the office, we spent hours together going through everything, sifting out the treasures from the stuff. It has been a grieving process for us both, but it has had its moments of humor. Mom was not the most organized of women, and we have found some odd things in unlikely places.

One of the most delightful discoveries was stuffed in the back of a laundry room closet: this old grocery bag from a store that has been gone for twenty years, filled with your letters. This was no surprise to us, really. Your letters were enjoyed by all of us through the years—so full of news and the daily events that comprise our lives—and we all read them with pleasure. A letter from Rose was a big deal to my mother, and she announced each one's arrival with delight.

"I got a letter from Rose," was an indication of a happy day.

That my mother collected your letters was no surprise to us—I had even seen the bag before—but you must admit that the volume is astonishing. But more, they are a measure of your devoted friendship.

We know that these are not all of your letters. From time to time, Mom would go on a short-lived decluttering binge, and many things would be cast off. It would have been fun to have them all dating back to that first one after our move to Michigan. But even so, the bag was only the beginning. As we went through the house, we would find your letters tucked away in pockets, in bureau drawers, in boxes of bank statements, and as bookmarks. It was a source of amusement to us in our work to come upon them in unexpected places. "I've found another Rose letter" became our running joke.

So, forgive us for running out of sorting steam, but we are sending you what we found, more or less unedited. If you come upon a bank statement, please destroy it. But I hope you find these letters a pleasurable record of your life and your friendship with my mother. I know she loved you. And, so do we both. My mother was extraordinarily lucky to have a friend like you.

49

THE INTRICACIES OF CASUAL CONVERSATION

I am on a first name basis with the people at our local hardware store. I am there sporadically but often, and they have patiently, and without one note of patronization, advised me on various topics ranging from the correct size of a wall anchor to replacing an outlet. They greet me like an old friend when I come in, and this minor element of small-town life cheers me.

The frequency of my visits has increased recently for various reasons, so our conversations have taken on a serial quality, generally picking up where we left off. I was standing at the register this week, piling up my purchases. "Will this be all?" I was asked politely. I struggled perfunctorily with myself and lost.

"And a package of Chuckles."

Chuckles are a candy I know from my childhood, rarely seen anymore, at least in the Midwest. They are an oblong package of five flat squares of gum drop style candy with little ridges shaped into them and coated with a crystal layer of sugar. They are always laid out in the same order: red, yellow, black, orange, green. I'm not sure when the hardware store started carrying them. But I first started noticing them this summer, when I was making frequent visits for items to prepare my late mother's house for sale.

After our business was finished, I stood chatting and opened up my package of Chuckles as I did so. Watching me, the owner said:

"You know, no one who buys those can ever leave the store without opening the package."

"Really?"

"There's something about their connection to childhood, I think. It's powerful." She paused for a moment, recollecting. "One guy who comes in stands at the counter to eat them so he can throw away the package here and his wife won't know."

"Maybe it's better as a guilty pleasure."

"So many things are."

There was a moment of silence as I ate the first Chuckle.

"Which is your favorite?" the owner wanted to know. She pointed to the clerk. "He never eats the orange ones."

"Really?" I was aghast. Orange is one of the best flavors.

"I find the orange ones hidden behind the counter." She looked sideways at her assistant.

The clerk was not in the least abashed. "I start to eat them and then forget about them."

"You have to eat them in order," I said. "It's a cardinal rule."

This interested them, and they both looked at me.

"You must be right about the childhood thing. I've been eating them this way since I was small. Green first. And then each flavor in the order they're laid out in the package. Because the best one is the red one, and you have to save the best for last."

As I thought about this piece of childish philosophy, I suddenly realized that it was more complicated, and I hadn't been aware of it until this moment. I spoke slowly as my awareness of the process unfolded from my subconscious.

"And you can't bite them right away. You have to let them melt in your mouth until all the sugar is gone, and then you bite into the little ridges very carefully. Then you can chew the pieces. But it's better if you let them slowly melt in your mouth."

"It's a childhood ritual," commented the clerk.

I nodded, thinking about the oddities of the mind, and how this leftover from my very early life could still be, unconsciously, part of my behavior. Another customer walked in, and we all went on with our day.

Somehow, the conversation came up with my friend later on.

She listened, and then she said:

"How long have you been doing this?"

"All my life."

"No. I mean eating the Chuckles. You don't eat candy."

I thought about it.

"I don't know. All summer, I guess. I'm not used to eating sugar, and they make me feel terrible afterward, but I can't resist. It's weirdly comforting."

"So you're eating a childhood candy, using a childhood ritual, as you work on fixing up your late mother's house. You don't need a degree in psychology to understand what's going on here."

"I guess not."

Hardware stores are interesting places. I've always thought so.

50

I SEE YOU NEVER

There is a short story by Ray Bradbury, the underrated master of American literature, that I read long ago. In it, Mr. Ramirez, an illegal immigrant and tenant of Mrs. O'Brien, is being taken away to be deported. He is a good man, and she likes him, but she is unable to help him in the face of the law. At the last moment, desperately, he cries out to her, "'Oh, Mrs. O'Brien! I see you never! I see you never!'" After he is gone, the woman starts to go on with her interrupted dinner, when she suddenly puts down her knife and fork, painfully struck by the realization that she will never see Mr. Ramirez again.

In winding up the details of my late mother's estate, there are large griefs and small ones. Each time I come back from her house, I am spent from the turmoil of emotion. There are so many things to do, the paperwork, the bills, the wrapping, the packing, and the decisions about what remnants of my parents lives to keep and what to abandon. It is heavy work. I never liked the house itself, but the finality of each step of the parting beats on the walls of my heart.

The house will be sold tomorrow, so I was there yesterday to meet the movers. The mailman, whom I have known for decades, was on his way to deliver a package across the street, and he stopped to talk. He is a kind man, always smiling, and he delivered mail to me in my own small house when I lived in that town, as well as to my parents. I haven't lived on his route for many years, but when we see each other we exchange pleasantries. He is, as a friend of mine likes to say, one of my life's cast of characters. He doesn't have a major part, but he has played in many small pleasant scenes, and his cheerful interactions have given me some of the happy little ordinary moments of everyday life.

Our conversation was light, and he enquired about the house. As we parted, we shook hands for the first and only time, and I said to him something I don't think I've ever said to anyone before: "I will probably never see you again." I had to turn away quickly to hide my feelings.

The finality broke hard, and I cried all the way up to the house.

I don't even know his name.

51

A THANKSGIVING FOR ORPHANS

Thanksgiving is my favorite holiday. I love the starkness of late fall, the sense of the beginning of things, filled with the anticipation of the holidays and the beauty of the coming winter. Ever since I have had my own household, I have filled my house with guests for Thanksgiving, joking that I was always on the lookout for holiday orphans.

But this year, for the first time, there will be no guests. I will make a traditional dinner, but it will only be my husband and me. For the first time, we are both orphans ourselves, and I don't have the energy to put up a cheerful front when the absence of so many people we loved will be so fully felt. Last year, on my mother's last Thanksgiving, I could fill the absence with the special care of her. She was the last man standing. Now she is gone.

Of those who used to grace our table annually, we have lost four.

You would think that in middle age, the loss of a parent would not hurt so much, but that is only what you would think until it happens to you. Every memory now is fraught with the poignancy of passing time, and the changing human geography of our lives. My dear friend, who lost her mother recently, said to me the other day: remember when we were kids, and no one ever died?

I see now how age can bring melancholy, with every new occasion or holiday memory colored by the loss of those who once celebrated with you, the loss of your old life, your old self, the family you always had.

But this is not the proper way to live. Each day is meant to be embraced with hope and joy. To do otherwise is a form of sinfulness.

Today will be hard, a deliberate pause to remember and mourn, and then to shed the old skin of grief.

Hope begins again tomorrow.

52

JOYS OF THE SEASON

Dear Secret Santa,

First, I want to thank you for reading my blog. I need all the readers I can get.

Second, I want to thank you for the package of Chuckles I found in my mailbox yesterday morning. My husband handed me the envelope after he had opened it accidentally and recognized for whom the gift must have been intended. The message inside said: "Merry Christmas from your Secret Santa."

I was in the middle of vacuuming out the car so human beings could sit in the back without acquiring full coats of fur, but I opened the package and ate them immediately. Green one first, red one last, all in the proper order. They were slightly frozen and chewier than usual. Delicious.

It was a lovely surprise, Santa. I am grateful.

My love to you, whoever you are.

And, of course, Merry Christmas!

53

OLD FRIENDS

My late mother had a good friend whom she admired greatly. Blanche will be 108 years old in February, and she still lives alone in her own house. She gets her hair done weekly, dresses beautifully, and is generally in good health.

A year or so ago, I stopped by to deliver my mother's birthday gift to Blanche while my mother, then 90, waited in the car. I spoke to Blanche and to her daughter, and, accustomed to my mother's deafness, used my opera singer voice.

"You don't have to yell at me," said Blanche, with great dignity. "I am not deaf."

"I'm sorry. My mother is," I said apologetically.

"I know," said Blanche.

I picked up my mother's mail this week, and in the piles of junk mail and solicitations for donations for every charitable cause imaginable, I found a Christmas card from Blanche, signed in a firm, lovely hand.

Somehow, in my mother's small town, the news of her death six months ago had not reached Blanche, and it had not occurred to me to call her personally.

I will have to write a note this week. I dread bearing the news that will reduce the small circle of contemporaries for this remarkable old lady. (If contemporary is the right word. At 91, my mother could have been her daughter.) My mother used to say how hard it was when all your friends were gone. How lonely. Blanche is accustomed to death, no doubt, but each loss must surely add up, and one hesitates to add weight to so many years.

I am wondering if I should wait until after Christmas, but perhaps that would be a form of selfishness.

It's difficult to know. But probably sooner is better.

54

DOG JOY

Whenever I can, I like to take our dogs for a walk in a particular woods. We have to drive there, and the dogs know the place by sight. They also know the difference between when we are actually going there and when we are only driving past. Even if I haven't said anything, when the turn signal goes on at a particular intersection, they know we are going to the woods. But usually, just to give them the pleasure of anticipation, I say to them, "Do you want to go to the woods?" and they immediately begin to sing with joy.

Moses, who until recently had been the least vocal of the two, is the most expressive where the woods are concerned. It's his favorite place. He starts with warbles in a rich baritone, but as we get closer he switches to yips in an increasingly higher tessitura, until he reaches soprano range in keeping with his rising excitement. Pete joins in with his characteristic alto. By the time I can get around to open the door, they are tumbling over one another to get out and run, barking as if they were on the hunt. Sometimes there are deer, or squirrels, and the dogs tear after them, disappearing into the hills out of sight. If I am patient (meaning not too cold) I let them come back when they want to. But if I whistle, they always come. I can hear them coming usually before I see them, and they arrive at my feet bustling with joy and pride.

Their happiness delights me and is often the best part of the day.

55

THE FAULT IS NOT IN THE STARS BUT IN OURSELVES

I have many gaps in my education, and I do not spend as much time as I ought to in filling them. The list is long and daunting.

Last night, when I walked with the dogs for the last time before bed, I looked up with wonder at the many more stars that are visible here on the Island, and, for the thousandth time, I felt ashamed that I could not name more of them. I have often meant to learn more of the constellations, but my progress is slow, and I am easily distracted by daily life.

Tonight, after much nagging from the dogs, I interrupted my reading to take them out into the night. On All Saints Day, with Pete and Moses joyously romping around me, I walked in the dark, speaking the names of my beloved dead. My mother; my father; my grandmother whom I knew; my grandfather whom I did not; the grandfather whom I knew; the grandmother whom I did not. My cousin, Keith; my Uncle Bill; my Uncle Ken; my school friend, Dawn; my friend, Bill; my mother-in-law, Kay; my honorary parents, Tom and Carole; and many others.

The dogs, who know my moods but not their meaning, ran to and fro, happy merely to be outside and with me. The sound of the waves on the lake was slow and steady. The winds were still after yesterday's wild weather.

Coming back up the path to the house, I looked up and realized that along with Ursa Major, there was another constellation I thought I knew in the shape of a W. It was, I think, Cassiopeia, located almost above our heads. The crescent moon, which must be waxing, was large as it was setting into the Lake below the crest of the bluff.

The dogs were as indifferent to the stars as the stars are to human lives. But knowing things is both a burden and a gift.

Tonight, when the souls of the dead are closest to us, may they rest; may they find peace; may the momentary beauties of their lives enhance eternity. World without end. Amen.

56

MOVING FORWARD

So, I have been engrossed in writing my next book, and then, this past month, immersed in a long and lovely visit from family.

But it has been the writing, mainly, that has engaged my entire heart and mind these past eighteen months. I have done nothing but go to work and write and, in the process, have ignored everything from friendships to laundry and all the common attentions to little things that comprise daily life. The weight of the deadline was heavy, and I simply did not have room in my head for anything else.

With the novel finished and in the hands of my editor, I have begun the process of digging out. I am attempting to renew my connections to the people I care about, to do the laundry, sort the mail and the many dropped details of life. The neglect has left a field strewn with casualties.

So, yesterday, alone and unscheduled for the first time in almost a year, I sat down to re-engage with my other writing. In the process, I re-read old blog postings and began, with some dismay, to discover how heavily the theme of death marches through my thoughts. I suppose that I have played out my grief in my writing more thoroughly than I had realized.

I heard someone say recently that we get sadder as we get older. That is clearly the natural trend of things. We are battered by life, by the struggles and the losses, and as we lose our people, we become less sheltered from it all. The multiple losses these past eight years have made me acutely aware of my own mortality, and it looms.

This is the struggle. I look back at my parents' lives, at the lives of my godmother, my 95-year-old aunt—who is still with us and struggling herself to find meaning in her loneliness—and I wish I had known enough to listen more closely to them. I did try. I did my best. I still do. But then we get caught up in our own lives. And that is right, too.

I am sure there is a quote from Marcus Aurelius to fit here.

So, anyway. Getting older and facing loss requires strength and courage and determination and a whole lot of cussedness. We cannot succumb to despair. We must accept the new landscapes of our lives and get on with it. Not with sadness, but with joy and gratitude and, well, cussedness.

Damned if I won't be happy today.

57

THE MEMORIES OF OBJECTS

I had a birthday in February. Not a big one, just an I'm-glad-to-have-another-year-on-earth one. It was also my first birthday without my mother, so there was a tinge of melancholy around the edges. Perhaps more than a tinge. My husband's gift was tickets to a concert I had wanted to see, and even though I had asked to go, by the time I got home from work, I wanted to put on my pajamas and sit by the fire with the dogs. We went anyway. And in one of life's great lessons, in not going, we would have missed something irreplaceable and rare.

The concert was the 300th anniversary of the Lipinski Stradivarius. It's the same violin that made all the headlines last year when it was stolen and subsequently recovered. The violin is called the Lipinski because it was once owned by Karol Lipinski, a virtuoso performer renowned throughout 19th century Europe.

All of the music on the program was music that had been played on or written for the Lipinski Stradivarius. The last piece was a well-known quartet by Robert Schumann, written for Karol Lipinski. In the introduction to the piece, the violinist, Frank Almond, spoke about the history of the music. It was a favorite piece of mine, known since childhood. After he had finished speaking and the music began, it suddenly struck me. I was listening to music played on the same instrument that probably first played those notes. The violin had been in the presence of Robert Schumann and, no doubt, his beautiful and gifted wife, the pianist Clara Wieck Schumann, and perhaps their friend and her admirer, Johannes Brahms.

It was a moment of acute awareness of the transitory nature of human life and of connection to these real people, who had existed before only as names and figures of history. The Schumanns are long dead. They had tragic lives, but the longing and intensity of their love for one another give them an immortal status, even without their respective musical genius. And here was this object, this inanimate, yet fully animated instrument, which was here to bear witness to lives long gone—Stradivari, Lipinski, the Schumanns, Brahms—now remembered not by their own intimate and personal consciousness, but by their creations. Their bodies are dust, but the expressions of their hands and minds live on for the benefit of civilization 300 years later, 180 years later, and for as long as human beings still cherish such things. May that be forever.

It was a memorable birthday.

58

MY AUNT RUTH

Everyone else knows her as Barbie, but my mother called her Ruth, so we do, too. She is my late mother's older sister, and she will be 96 on April 15th, God willing.

Up until Tuesday, she lived alone in her own little house, trusting in the support of those who love her, including friends and neighbors, to look out for her if she needed help. At 3 am on Tuesday morning, she woke up and knew that something was terribly wrong. She called her friend, Randy, able to utter only one word: "Come." And come he did. He called the ambulance and waited with her while he held her hand, his face only a few inches from hers, speaking quietly to her.

If we have angels on earth, he is one.

She had had a stroke. My sister and I made an emergency trip to upstate New York to see her. We kissed her, and held her hand, and prayed with her, and told her we love her.

"How did I get to be so old?" she asked me. Her speech is thick from the stroke, and it is difficult to understand everything.

I leaned in close to gather her words. "But inside, you feel the same as when you were six," I said.

She nodded. "Just the same."

She is speaking better and has agreed to go into rehab so she can go back to her little house. When I kissed her goodbye, she was returning to her feisty self. I think you have to be feisty to live to be 95.

It gives me hope.

59

BIG FUR HAT

In her last years, my mother was always cold, and she complained about it regularly. She always admired ladies she saw with mink hats, and since she rarely asked for anything, a few years ago, I decided to get her one for Christmas.

After some searching, I found a company called Big Fur Hats, or something to that effect. I spent a ridiculous amount of money—had she known, my frugal mother would have been horrified—to buy her one. I was pretty pleased with myself when I presented it to her, but I could see instantly that she did not like it. Gamely, she tried it on, and I think she wore it once or twice, but she hated it, I could tell.

The Big Fur Hat (BFH) is mine now, and it is an essential part of my equipment on Washington Island. I don't care what I look like there, which is part of the fun, I admit, so I wear it when the dogs and I go for our walks. I look ridiculous, but it keeps my head warm without interfering with my hearing. It is a lifesaver, especially when the wind is blowing. Without it, I would be forced to shorten our walks, the source of the dogs' joy and my inspiration.

A few weeks after blowing all that money on the unloved BFH, I found a vintage mink hat in a consignment store for $12. My mother loved it.

That's mine now, too.

There may be a lesson here, but I'm not sure what it is.

60

MOUSE TRAP

We'd been having a butter situation. I mean, I am one of those people who scoffs at the avoidance of butter. Avoidance of wheat? Fine. Sugar? Okay. Salty crackers? Reluctantly. Dairy products? Sigh. Okay. Alcohol? On weeknights. And even for long periods of weekends. But butter is essential to the flavor of vegetables, and if I'm going to eat vegetables, or eggs, or...lots of things, there must be butter. Not a whole stick or anything, but enough. I am willing to eat healthy things. I have my blueberries and kale daily. But we all have our limits to sacrifice.

I make omelets a lot in the morning, and these require butter. They used to require a special, expensive omelet pan, but it's gone now. Another story. Anyway, I'm the only cook in our household, so I'm fairly acquainted with the butter usage in our house, and I suddenly noticed that we were going through an awful lot of butter. But I'm busy, kind of absentminded, and not always fully attentive to the tasks at hand, so when the butter ran out, I didn't think that much about it. I'd just grab another stick and put it on a fresh butter dish in its place on an open shelf, next to the stove, about five feet up.

This had been going on for some time. But eventually, the light dawned on me, even while in the midst of plotting out a book. I knew I'd opened a fresh stick of butter at dinner, but the next morning, there wasn't any. Odd, I thought. I asked my husband, "Did you use any butter?" He hadn't, as I had known. I turned to look at my dogs, lying patiently nearby, and they gazed back with the usual proportion of adoration, hope, and pseudo-guilelessness.

Pete is nearly twelve, we think, and not inclined toward much in the way of vigor these days. When inspired, he can still run like the wind. But inspiration is more of a once-a-day thing—during one of our walks in the woods, for example, or to chase off a particularly arrogant turkey. But he doesn't jump much anymore. We have to lure him with treats to get him to come up on the bed to cuddle.

This left Moses, our 125-pound German Shepherd, who has been known to jump horse hurdles in agility classes and has an intellectual capacity superior to that of a small child. He held my gaze and thumped his tail affectionately. He is a well-trained and, like both my dogs, very well-loved. He knows the rules. He lies peacefully nearby while we eat. He takes treats gently from fingers. He asks to go out. He comes when he's called, crashing thunderously through the underbrush when drawn away from chasing a deer, to sit, panting, at my feet. He stays where he's been told for long periods of time in unfamiliar environments. He is certified to go to schools and hospitals, and it is only my own schedule that keeps him from being certified as a therapy dog. He is my heart and soul.

I'd like to point out, too, that my dogs are well-fed. In addition to ridiculously expensive grain-free organic dog food, they eat fresh chicken or turkey every day, eggs on occasion, human-grade, freeze-dried chicken hearts and liver as treats, and large, lovely, smoked beef bones from the grocery store butcher shop.

The suspicion in my mind was fully formed. "Listen," I said to my husband, who needs prompting to do so. "You are my witness. I'm putting out a full stick of butter this morning." He was skeptical. "That shelf is pretty high up."

We went our separate ways to work.

He called around lunch time to tell me that the butter was gone.

A little butter isn't bad for dogs. But too much fat is, causing pancreatitis, which is pretty serious.

The next morning, with some trepidation, I put out a fresh stick of butter. On the counter, I put a mouse trap and covered it with a dish towel, a method I had learned from our dog trainer but had never tried before. It is not suitable for small dogs, but for big dudes like Moses, it merely startles and stings. Nervously, I tried the trap on my fingers. It hurt.

When we came home, the trap and towel were on the

floor. The butter was untouched and has not been touched since. We caught a very big mouse that day. A very big, very smart mouse.

61

STAR-CROSSED LOVE

I had to stop at a store today to return something, a task I detest, but which you might think was among my very favorite activities given how often I find myself doing it.

The clerk and I started chatting, and, one thing leading to another, I mentioned my two dogs in the car. "What kind of dogs?" she asked. I gave my standard answer: Pete, an Indiana Spotted Dog (Pete is of indeterminate breed, but with a speckled coat that looks like granite), and Moses, a German Shepherd.

Her attention was instantly riveted by the words "German Shepherd."

"I had a German Shepherd," she said. "But I had to put him down." I felt a wave of sympathy. The shortness of dogs' lives is a looming loss for those of us who love them, and the thought of it can shatter me if I linger on it.

She knew what I have learned: that there is something different about German Shepherd Dogs, no matter what other kinds of dogs you have had or how much you have loved them. I told her what the vet told me when Moses was a tiny puppy: "Nothing and no one on earth will ever love you as much as a German Shepherd will."

Her eyes filled with tears, and mine did, too. She told me how true that was, and how smart her dog had been, and what a clever jailbreak artist he was. She told me that even when his hip dysplasia had made it impossible for him to walk, she had cared for him until his pain became too much.

She seemed so sad. When I suggested that somewhere in the world there was a dog who desperately needed someone like her to love him, she shook her head. No. She could never endure that loss again. It was too much.

The store was busy, and people were waiting for her attention, but I wished I could have taken her out for a cup of coffee and brought her over to meet Moses and Pete, waiting patiently, if a bit odoriferously, in the car.

I have writing to do, and I have to go to Washington for work tomorrow, and I don't know how I'm going to get everything done before I leave the house at 5:30 in the morning.

But Moses and Pete and I are going for a ramble. Life is all about priorities.

62

INTRODUCTION OF ALEXANDER MCCALL SMITH

We live in troubled times. Although in the West we have lives of comfort and ease beyond the dreams of any other era of humanity, we wake, I believe, most days, with the sense that something has gone deeply wrong.

And then we realize that our iPhones are safe in the next room.

Modern life, in its material richness, is often plagued by anxiety. And when we have read the dire stories in the news, witnessed the crudeness and vulgarity of mainstream culture, and exhausted our capacity for cruelty and vituperation on Twitter, our minds and souls are in desperate need of an escape. If we have any sense at all, we turn to books as our refuge.

Alexander McCall Smith is the master of escapist literature. I use that term with deep admiration. It requires firm principles, deep courage, and a steadfast heart to look around and find joy and things to laugh about. Perhaps it also requires a bit of desperation.

His books, however charming, express both a deeply

held moral philosophy and biting social satire. And whether it's Isabel Dalhousie in her beautiful house in Edinburgh, Mma Ramotswe in Botswana, or seven-year-old Bertie reluctantly practicing yoga at 44 Scotland Street, his protagonists have a firm determination to do what's right: to be honest, to express and appreciate beauty, to find meaning, and most particularly, to be kind.

The humor can be subtle or riotous, but the beauty and warmth and rich value of everyday people living everyday lives of meaning and virtue is at the core of every book. And today—indeed, in any era—that is a powerful and important thing.

Escapist literature is a banner of hope in a dark world. And, as Mma Ramotswe says: "… it is possible to change the world, if one is determined enough, and if one sees with sufficient clarity just what has to be changed."

Our guest, tonight, is an extraordinarily prolific novelist and story writer, over the course of many years. He is the author of multiple series—including my favorite, *Portuguese Irregular Verbs*, which features the hapless Herr Professor Doktor Moritz-Maria von Igelfeld—and along with this new addition to his *Number One Ladies Detective Agency* series, has another new children's book about to be published in Britain. He is the recipient of many honors, and a Commander of the British Empire.

The truth is, he needs no introduction to any of you, but I really wanted to meet him.

63

WHAT WRITERS DO WHEN THEY SHOULD BE WRITING

Decide to take dogs for walk.
Look for sunglasses in purse.
Go outside to see if sunglasses are on porch.
Talk to neighbors for two hours over fence.
Look for sunglasses on bedside table.
Pick up t-shirt on bedroom floor.
Notice box of new beach towels in guest room.
Put away new beach towels.
Look for sunglasses in car.
Make grocery list.
Recharge computer.
Check e-mail. Nothing from anyone.
Look for sunglasses in tote bag.
Wonder if sunglasses are still at bookstore from last night.
Call bookstore.
Wonder if sunglasses are at restaurant from last night.
Call restaurant.
Look for sunglasses in car again, focusing under seats.
Talk to friend on phone.

Look at plot map. Notice holes in plot.
Ponder death.
Empty purse on floor looking for sunglasses. Find emptied bottle of zinc tablets in bottom.
Clean out purse. Pick off lint from zinc tablets. Return to bottle.
Accidentally call bookstore from last week. Chat with proprietor.
Decide to write blog post.
Look for sunglasses in car again, focusing on trunk.
Stare at blog screen.
Send irritable e-mail to online company that keeps sending surveys that flash at you when you're trying to think.
Look for sunglasses in tote bag again.
Find two-day-old *New York Times* in tote bag.
Do crossword puzzle in *New York Times.*
Walk path from car to door, hoping to find sunglasses in grass.
Rub tummy of Dog One.
Stare at blog screen.
Rub tummy of Dog Two.
Look for sunglasses in different tote bag. Find sunglasses.
Resolve to carry fewer tote bags.
Don't write a single thing all morning.
Decide it's too hot to take dogs for walk. Swimming would be better.
Look for sunglasses.

64

THE MOST BEAUTIFUL DAY IN THE WORLD

One of my favorite writers, the melancholy anthropologist Loren Eiseley, wrote an essay called "The Most Perfect Day in the World." In it, he describes a day when, utterly impoverished and riding freight trains across the country, he and a friend stopped in a small town on a sunny day, pooled their resources to buy a case of grape soda, and laid on the grass in the shade of a big tree all day, drinking soda and watching the clouds. This notion of perfection would not suit everyone, but it strikes me as a fine expression of the pure enjoyment of living, when time stops, and you can live in this one moment, freed from fear and worry.

Today, I am home from the office, ostensibly to proof my manuscript. But I have not done much work. It is a delightfully cool, breezy June morning, the first time sunshine has combined with the full fresh bloom of early summer. The dogs and I lolled on the grass before attacking the long list of procrastination—I mean errands—on my list. I walked in the garden where the irises are an edible deep purple, the pink roses are in bud, and the peonies are tight balls waiting to burst. I rambled out to the garage to find the loppers to prune the dead branches from the climbing rose on the arbor and wrestled them to the ground without too many thorn pricks. It is impossible to breathe in the air on day like this without experiencing a deep sense of wonder and gratitude. This is how I would like to spend my mornings forever.

But the day's beauty makes a hard contrast to the suffering happening in this moment in other parts of the world, of the people who are terrified, in pain, in fear of horrible deaths, in an agony of despair for their futures. Marcus Aurelius counsels the practice of these contrasts as a method of valuing each moment of life and of inuring the soul against too much dependence on the vagaries of fortune. I read his teachings, and I have tried to absorb them. And, I believe that we must all do what we can to make what we touch better, and to broaden our reach to others. But, I think modern angst is the result of our knowing too much about the suffering we cannot control. We are bombarded by war and poverty and natural disasters in every corner of the world, by the sufferings of people and the sufferings of animals. There is no doubt that we are meant to endure the suffering around us. But the suffering of the whole world is not a burden a human being can bear.

And so, Pete, Moses, and I will go out into the orchard and play ball in the sunshine, grateful for our blessings. But I will also offer my prayers for the souls in the dark, knowing that I am helpless to give them any relief. For us, it is the most beautiful day in the world.

It would be sinful to be sorry for that.

65

DELAYED GRATIFICATION

We are expecting a new puppy—a companion for Moses, and a respite, and new pupil, for Pete. My husband has misgivings about a third dog, and, although I generally keep them to myself, so do I. But, sadly, we won't have three forever, and I want Pete, the elder statesman, to help train the puppy.

The puppy will be a special one, like Moses, carefully bred to be healthy, smart, even-tempered, gentle, and sweet. Also, long-lived. These German Shepherds often live to be 13 or 14 years old, which is long for a big dog. Every day, I check the breeder's website to see the current puppies and look for news of the coming event. But today, I found out it won't be late fall, but early spring.

I am a little disappointed, but it gives me time to continue my ruminations on names. Leading contenders for now are Marcus Aurelius; St. Augustine; Herodotus (I know); and George.

Official dog names are usually pompous, with the kennel name in the possessive first, followed by the particular dog's name. Still, it's always possible to have fun with the form. With Peter and Moses, we have New Testament and Old Testament represented. But the truth is that Moses's name, although he is officially Moses, Prince of Egypt, was actually the result of my watching *The Ten Commandments* too frequently in my youth. I wanted to be able to shake my head sorrowfully and say, "Moses, Moses, Moses."

I'm kind of leaning toward George. But, I am open to suggestions. He's expected to be 140 pounds. He'll need something he can grow into.

66

ONE TINY LIGHT GOES OUT

We lost our two-week-old puppy today. It's not exactly clear what happened, but he died a terrible death, crushed.

We never held him, or knew him beyond his photographs, but we had named him. He was real. And, we were waiting to bring him home to us.

Loving anything means that you can be wounded by its loss, and we already loved this small creature, his soul shining with innocence.

I don't believe the universe is indifferent to miracles, no matter how small. His life seems, to me, wasted. But he lived. And somehow that matters.

I need to believe that for even the smallest life, the angels weep.

67

LIVING IN HOPE

We are in the queue again for a puppy. He has been born. He will be two weeks old tomorrow. We hope to pick him up and fly him home (on our laps) from Georgia on May 6th. He is a cousin, of some sort, of Moses.

My husband insists that his name will be St. Augustine the Younger. He gets to pick, since I picked Moses, but I am still lobbying for St. George the Dragon Slayer.

He will win.

Because my life needs a complication, albeit a delightful one.

68

MUSE

I have been procrastinating. It is a well-known but little understood phenomenon of the writing process.

Every writer procrastinates differently. My method is cleaning and decluttering my workspace and finishing up little tasks that distract me. Having a clear, open space and no little worries helps to clear my mind, and then the ideas that are spinning around my head in an inchoate mess suddenly coalesce into plot lines and sometimes into complete scenes. I know this process, but it is very hard to accept that I need to do it when I feel a deadline looming, and time slipping away from me.

The other night, I was driving home from some event and suddenly an entire line of development for the new book entered my mind, and I couldn't get my coat off fast enough to write it all down. It is an odd sequence, a departure from my usual style, and after a few days of musing over it, I put it down. It was risky, and it didn't fit the book. Maybe another book.

Then everything stopped. I couldn't write much. I

couldn't catch the wind that sails me through my writing. I sat at my desk, restlessly, unproductively, staring out the window, looking at YouTube videos, researching mammals and explosives (not together), and periodically going downstairs to see if I could alleviate my boredom by eating. Fortunately, knowing myself, I have purged my kitchen of these kinds of foods, and even though I am a novelist, drinking in the middle of the day does not normally appeal to me. I consumed a lot of tea and far too much coffee.

So, finally, I gave up. I stopped worrying about it and just got on with other tasks. I cleaned out a closet in the kitchen. I rearranged my office and made plans for new bookcases. I dusted under beds. I threw a small dinner party and took the dogs for walks.

This morning, I began my day before dawn, standing barefoot on the patio, loudly and frantically calling my dogs in—no doubt to the amusement of my neighbors, who were recovering from their New Year's Eve revelries—while a fairly large contingent of coyotes barked and yipped and howled somewhere very nearby.

Dogs safe, I sat drinking coffee and watching the turkeys begin their new year from their treetop berths, their big bulbous shapes silhouetted against the pink and orange sky.

All at once, the spinning stopped, and the words began again in my head. My refusal to accept the strange passage as part of the novel had shut me down. I suddenly knew that it did belong, and that it had to be the beginning of the book. And then everything began to fall in place in my mind, like the tumblers in a lock.

There it is. Not all of it. But the main points of it.

Time to write.

69

FOE OF COYOTE PAGANS

So, for those of you who have been kind enough to enquire, Book Three is coming along nicely. A small distraction will be developing soon, however. My husband and I will be traveling to Georgia next weekend to pick up our new puppy, St. Augustine. He is a cousin to Moses, and will, no doubt, be an annoyance to Pete.

My husband had had misgivings about a third dog until we caught a coyote stalking Pete, who, at thirteen, is spry and happy, but nearly stone deaf. Moses, a fearless opponent of coyotes, chased it off without missing a beat, with Pete being none the wiser. Coyote confrontation does not exactly make me happy, and I strive to prevent it, but it has worked out well for Pete. German Shepherds are often referred to as GSDs. In our house we use the term BSD, for Big Scary Dog.

Moses, however, needs a wingman.

The original St. Augustine, as you know, was the author of *City of God Against the Pagans*. At the moment, Auggie is more adorable than formidable and can't be allowed out by himself. But we think he may grow into his name. His father weighs 140 pounds.

70

PRAY FOR RUTH

Holy God, Heavenly Father.

I beg of You to forget the world. Forget that we sit on the brink of war and chaos. Forget that the last best hope of Mankind sits under the power of the unworthy. Lord God, Most Holy, Creator of Heaven and Earth, please sit with Barbara Ruth. Let her know Your love. Let her feel Your comfort. Let the embrace of Your angels surround and protect her in her fear and pain. Love her. Hold her in Your love, and let those of us who love her, too, comfort her in every possible way. In Jesus's name, I pray that I may be an instrument to her peace. Please, God, let me be a blessing to her, and let her know that she is not alone.

> *Keep watch, dear Lord, with those who work, or watch, or weep this night, and give your Angels charge over those who sleep. Give rest to the weary, Lord Christ. Soothe the suffering, pity the afflicted, bless the dying, and shield the joyous, all for Your love's sake.*
>
> —From *The Book of Common Prayer*

Amen.

71

FOR RUTH: A REMEMBRANCE

To everyone else she was Barbie, but since my mother called her Ruth, we did, too. I don't even know why.

Our Aunt Ruth will be buried on Friday in a rural cemetery in upstate New York, and we will not be there. She, my sister, Eileen, and I had discussed this. She was quite clear that she didn't want a fuss: no funeral; no flowers. So, as we all agreed, we spent our time and efforts while she needed them.

We were with her on her 95th birthday. On her 96th birthday, we couldn't come until the following weekend, so we sent her 96 roses and, combined with all the other flowers she received, her tiny house was so filled with flowers there was no place to set a coffee cup. I didn't make it for her 97th, but I took comfort in knowing that Eileen and her children were there.

Eileen, living nearer, visited Ruth more frequently than I. We made little visits together that always felt like pilgrimages, and I wept so often after saying goodbye, thinking each time would be the last, that I think I got complacent. It almost started to feel that she would always be there. But last week, we held her in our arms as she took her last breaths.

As we drove away from the hospice, I kept looking around me at the familiar landscape, thinking I would probably never come back. After a lifetime of trips to that cluster of little towns on the Hudson, it felt very strange. It was the end of more than her life. It was the end of an era in my own life, and the end of my family's history there. The shadows of my aunt's and my parents' young lives, of their hopes and dreams, and the young lives of their parents, are all left behind, with no one living there to meet them and remember.

When a celebrity dies, there is always a flurry of remembrance, while most of the rest of us disappear into obscurity. But in the end, it doesn't matter whether you are famous, and it doesn't matter whether you are perfect.

What matters is that you craft a life with what you are given. You make friends and lose them, you have your small pleasures, your personal triumphs, and your private tragedies.

It matters whether you did your best to struggle through, whether you were kind sometimes, whether you were generous sometimes, whether you handled your troubles with as much grace as you could muster, whether you found some love and gave some love. These are the things that give our lives meaning. And these are the things that deserve tribute, and remembrance, and a prayer.

Like my mother—her sister—Ruth was vibrant,

enthusiastic, adventurous, and also headstrong, stubborn, opinionated, and extraordinarily difficult. And like my mother, she took great pride in being difficult. Apparently, it's a family trait.

But she also had great love. She adored my Uncle Ken, and he adored her. They endured terrible tragedy together, but they always had each other. Not in a fluffy, romantic way, but in a difficult, holding it all together, we'll get through this kind of way. They had grit.

They travelled extensively throughout the United States and Canada, and they seemed always to be having fun. They once surprised me by appearing in Halifax, Nova Scotia, where a ship on which I was working as a singer had docked. They were so pleased with my delight at seeing them.

During World War II, on her way to Seattle to meet her husband's ship, Ruth was the survivor of a notorious train wreck. She decided not to go to the dining car at precisely the right moment. Many passengers died. She walked away.

Ruth could handle a gun, and she used to hunt and trap with her father to feed their family during the depression. She was a gifted seamstress and knitter and, until she lost her sight near the end, made countless caps for preemies at local hospitals and beautiful, intricate baby sweaters, and booties, and caps. I gave the last one to someone only this past summer.

When I married, she made me a full trousseau of dish-towels and placemats with matching napkins and crocheted tiny white lace snowflakes and beaded icicles for my Christmas tree. I still have them all—even the dish towels.

When Aunt Ruth's first husband, our Uncle Ken, died suddenly after many years of marriage, Eileen and Ruth and I went up to their little cabin in the Adirondacks to empty out the remnants of their life together. As a remembrance, Ruth gave me one of Ken's plaid flannel shirts, over whose torn pocket she had patched a red felt heart. I gave it back to her on her 95th birthday. She hadn't known I'd kept it, and she cried with delight to have it back.

She fell in love again at the age of 80 and married another lovely man, Al, who was both generous and kind. We have a picture of her and my mother on the night before the wedding, their arms around one another, laughing. Ruth was as beautiful as any younger bride, so filled with happiness. The rain came down in buckets, but it didn't matter.

To her sorrow, Aunt Ruth outlived Al, too. They only had a few years together.

My mother and Ruth were both beautiful young women, and like the princesses in the fairy tale, one was blonde and the other was dark. As she got older, Ruth was proud that her blonde hair had no gray in it. Last week at her bedside, as Eileen stroked her head, she reminded Ruth that even at 97, her hair was still blonde.

Eileen viewed Ruth as a second mother, and she was closer to Ruth than I. But when my mother was alive, Eileen and I split our duties. I lived close enough to help Mom.

Eileen lived close enough to help Ruth. We were so grateful, though, to have one another last week during the ordeal of Ruth's death. Neither of us could have endured it alone.

This tribute comes at my sister's urging. Aunt Ruth did not want an obituary, but since Ruth didn't always do what she was told, my sister and I are following her example. We come by our stubbornness honestly.

Ruth is the last of her generation in my family. My father and mother have already been gone, it seems, forever. For my sister and me, she has left another gap in our hearts, another hole in the landscape of our lives. She fought, she loved, she created, she struggled. And in this eternal and sometimes merciless universe, she mattered. Her loves mattered. Her struggles mattered. Her fierceness mattered. Her sorrows mattered. The people she lost matter. The lives she created matter.

We loved her. We love her still.

We will miss her always.

72

MISSING LINK

Shortly after my mother's death, about three years ago, my sister gave me a gift: a pair of earrings she had had made from my father's monogrammed sterling silver cuff links, still nestled in cream velvet in their original oval, purple velvet box. I was touched and delighted by them, excited to wear them, and to have this keepsake.

One winter afternoon, I wore them for the first time and went shopping with a friend. We had fun, wandering from one shop to the next and spending a fair amount of time trying on hand-knitted hats. I guess our ears were cold.

It was about an hour later that I realized I was wearing only one earring. The mood of the afternoon was instantly altered. I tried not to show how upset I was, reminding myself that it was just a thing. We retraced our steps, I went through all the hats, gently shaking them and looking for something caught in them. I crawled on the floor of the shop. Hopefully, I left my name and number with several of the stores we had been in, but I never heard from anyone. It was gone.

I never said anything to my sister. I put the one cufflink/earring away in its ancient purple velvet box and promised myself that someday I would have it made into a necklace. But I felt sick at the loss.

Yesterday was my birthday, and although I try hard to be grateful to be having a birthday, I spent the day fighting off a case of melancholy. I felt the passing of time, the shortening of the horizon, and a soft, persistent nostalgia for my late parents. Don't misunderstand: there were cards, and gifts, and flowers, and phone calls, greetings from friends and strangers, a snowstorm, and, best of all, an advance copy of my new novel in the mail. Nevertheless, I spent the day in an uncharacteristic lethargy, unable to accomplish much of anything.

Toward the end of the day, though, I bestirred myself to straighten our dark, cozy library for the evening. I had recently redone the room as a surprise for my husband and had emptied the shelves and cleared all the surfaces before and after I painted. The little brass tables had gotten wiped and polished, and even the bottles on the bar cart had been dusted. I oiled the wood. On Friday, our cleaning lady went over everything again, so it all sparkled.

I lit a fire and some candles, and I put on my favorite Beethoven piano sonata, which reminds me of my father's last days. Feeling both sorrowful and affectionate, I began stacking the week's collection of books and papers to make some room on the table, when something caught my eye. On the table—the table I had emptied and polished twice in the past week—was a small oval silver shape. It was an earring.

Unbelieving, I went to my bureau where the purple box was kept. The one earring was in the box. The other was in my hand.

I immediately texted my cleaning lady. Yes, she had found it in the couch and forgotten to say anything.

But here's the thing. In three years, the house has been cleaned many times. The couch has been vacuumed at least every other week. There is a perfectly rational explanation for how the earring got there. But it feels, to me, as if I had a visitation, and I can't help but believe that on this melancholy birthday, as I listened to the music that brings him so vividly to mind, my father reached through the weave of time. Warmed and happier, I wore the earrings last night, ate cake, and drank champagne.

Wisdom tells us not to put too much value in things, or to choose mysticism over reason. But sometimes when we don't expect it, everything shifts, the lines can blur, and the momentary mysteries we see instead make life's realities both rich and beautiful.

73

LETTER TO A POET 2

I was once again delighted to hear from you.

It is so interesting to hear the backstory on *String too Short to be Saved.* I only recently realized that Roger Angell was E.B. White's stepson. I have read several of his baseball books. How wonderful that your life has afforded you friendships with other important writers. That was the first book of yours that I bought—or perhaps, was given—back when I was in college. It's still here on my shelves, along with your other books, and two copies of *White Apples and the Taste of Stone.* At some point, I had forgotten I already had it, but one is a beautiful hardcover.

Earlier than that, I cut out and saved—and realized this morning that I still have in a manila file folder—"Polonius' Advice to Poets." I just re-read it, and it still makes me laugh. I have read that essay so many times over the years that I have come to use some of its lines as stock phrases that recur in my daily conversations. "My sister's funeral was boring, but I got a poem out of it;" the mockery of (badly) translated poetry: "the bamboo under the mountain-color mountain;" and most important: "Remember what matters." I did not remember Polonius' advice to "write to poets and critics you admire, and some will write you back," but I have apparently internalized it all the same—just getting a late start. Coincidentally, the same college friend who probably gave me *String too Short* also most definitely gave me that essay and introduced me to baseball.

My husband leaves tomorrow for British Columbia on a business trip, so it will just be me and the dogs for the next few days. I will start by digging out my office and getting it comfortable again (my go-to writing procrastination tool), and then spend all next week working on my essays. Most are already written; it is a question of organization, editing, and culling (which, I guess, is editing).

I enjoy hearing what you know of Reuel. I think I may have met Polly but only vaguely recall.

So, you have abandoned port. How on earth can you get through any English novel without it? I don't love it, I admit, but wine in general—or, on dire occasions or very happy ones, bourbon—is a thing I have tried to give up, but never for very long. I went for a period when I gave up alcohol every Lent, but I got tired of using God as an excuse to diet and switched to giving myself unpleasant but wholesome reading assignments.

At the moment, I am reading Thucydides, re-reading Jane Austen's *Emma*, and picking through a bit of theology here and there. I know this sounds ridiculous, but I never really appreciated Auden until recently, so I've been reading him a lot and that's a sort of thoughtful haze over everything else. I never know where ideas will come from, so I'm happy to burrow through just about anything that isn't gruesome, but lately I'm finding all the war histories depressing. A little P.G. Wodehouse now and again is a good thing.

I am struggling to build my followers on Twitter, which, apparently, is *de rigueur* for book marketing, but eats up a lot of brain space. Most people there just want to be hideously cruel or fill up their heads with marshmallow goo. I find myself watching compulsively to see how my remarks are being followed and, in a flash, the hour is wasted, and I've read nothing edifying or encouraging and written absolutely nothing. It's a dead end, this stuff. "Remember what matters."

Anyway, with rain coming this week and being on my own, there are many interludes of paw washing and indoor ball playing in my future, still not writing, but all better uses of time than Twitter. Three dogs are so many more than two, and that 105-pound puppy is a bit of a handful. He is never tired. They are good company, though, for when I'm out here in The Sticks on my own. Together, they add up to more than 280 pounds worth of dog, and one, at least, looks as if he would eat all comers, and not cheerfully. I always feel safe.

I look forward to your book of essays and hope you'll share the news of the great-grandchild upon his or her arrival. Take care of yourself.

74

SKUNKED

So, at 4:56 p.m. yesterday, four minutes before my you-can-stop-working-now alarm went off, I was done. My husband was away, I had worked all day, and I was a little stir crazy. So were the dogs.

I combed my hair, put on some lipstick, and decided to go to the local farmers market to see if there was anything tempting. The dogs had already had their big walk of the day, but it was cool and cloudy, so they could come along and sit in the car if I stopped. That way, they wouldn't sulk at being left behind.

We all piled into the car, but when we got there, everybody had already gone. I needed to see the sky, so we went for a little drive. After some random driving around, I ended up at the grocery store. Not as good as the farmers market, but I'm always happy with a fresh rotisserie chicken.

As I returned to the car ten minutes later, I opened the hatch to put the groceries in the trunk. Moses was leaning his face on the backseat looking soulfully at me. "Oh, you big baby," I said. "You are such a good dog. I know what you want." He sighed, his eyes never leaving my face. "Okay. Just one little spin around the woods. Would you like that?"

So, we went to the woods. I in my new jeans and new suede espadrilles (I know) and dogs in their usual attire. The woods have trails that make successive circles with intersecting paths. One long route around would make everyone happy.

As I walked, I was very pleased with myself for having made this decision. I had needed this as much as the dogs, but they especially deserved something extra nice for having been so patient all day. The sun had come out for a bit, and it was a beautiful night.

Why is it that when I get all sentimental and self-congratulatory, something bad always happens?

Pete is always the pack instigator. He's the one who ran off the path to sniff at something interesting. Moses immediately followed, and Auggie galloped after them with his adolescent enthusiasm. At first, I thought it was a routine disgusting thing, and then I thought it was a squirrel because I could see the white tail flashing. It was not a squirrel. Squirrels do not have white tails.

Thank God, Auggie listened to me and did not get close. Pete, too, managed to get away. Who knows how. But Moses, who is particularly fond of squirrels in a way that squirrels don't quite appreciate, got a full-frontal spray of skunk. I think he must have gotten a mouthful of it. I was so concerned about getting them away from there that

I barely attended to his misery, which was profound. But by the time we ran back to the car, he seemed better.

Let me tell you that skunk smells much, much, much, much, much, much worse than you think. My dogs have had minor skunk encounters, so I had been lured into thinking that these situations are not all that bad. I was wrong. It was a very long five-minute drive home.

Then began the fun part.

Today we did a re-treatment with the anti-skunk enzyme, which is pretty good, except for the fact that you can't just spray it on a dog's face, where the worst smell is. Then we will wash Moses again. And probably again. And we will wash all the towels and things with the enzyme too. If that doesn't work, the towels will have to go.

Possibly we will repeat the process. I may also buy some tomato juice for his face. Maybe tomato paste.

I suppose I should be grateful that I only have one skunky dog, not three.

Did I mention my car? And the suede espadrilles?

It wasn't until later that I noticed the lump on Moses's leg. Skunk bite. Vet visit. Rabies booster. Antibiotics. Rotisserie chicken dinner for Moses. Wine for me. Possibly bourbon.

I'm not sure this counts as procrastination for the novel, but the results are the same.

75

HE'S ALL RIGHT

After multiple treatments, Moses still smelled like skunk around his eyes and muzzle. I couldn't put any of the harsher treatments near his eyes, so we went with the old-fashioned method of tomato paste.

Moses made it quite clear that this was beneath his dignity, but after he had wiped his face on Pete and splattered tomato paste all over Auggie, he contented himself with licking off some of the residue. He got several very big pieces of chicken for his patience. And he actually smells better too.

Meanwhile, I think we have his Halloween costume in the bag. The fierce dark eyes. The teeth. The red war paint against a dark background. The look of loathing. He would make a Sith Warrior to terrify the most stalwart heart.

76

SOUVENIR

My mother outlived my father by several years, and when she died, my sister and I faced the Sisyphean task of cleaning out their house. This included going through my father's shop in the basement and in the garage, where he did everything from making wooden lamp bases on his lathes, to machining new parts for his car, to carrying out scientific experiments. I'm fairly certain that he never threw anything away. Nothing. What is more, he had an extensive collection of things that had belonged to my grandmother and my great-grandparents. Apparently, none of them ever got rid of anything. And it wasn't only stuff, either—although my father had a depression era penchant for saving anything that might someday come in handy—but it was one-hundred-fifty-year-old mahogany chairs, oriental rugs, sterling silver, a family bible, photographs of five generations, and more.

For my sister and me, each decision to keep or discard bore an emotional weight that devastated us both. It took some months, and we were weary in heart and soul both during the task and for a long while after. Frankly, it would have been much easier for us if my parents had followed the contemporary urge to "declutter." But if they had, so much would have been lost.

The word souvenir comes from the French: a thing that makes you remember. And, perhaps that is what exhausted us so much. Every little item we found had a memory attached. My mother's battered ancient fruitcake tin, where she kept her needles, pins, and thread, and which was always hidden under her chair in the living room. My father's homemade work aprons that had so often been our gifts to him on Father's Day or his birthday; his navy insignia; his little leather notebooks where he kept lists of books he wanted to read, recordings he wanted to buy, the names, ranks, stations, and bunk numbers of everyone on his ship during World War II, poems he wanted to remember, a recipe for applejack eggnog. Even my grandmother's things were still enmeshed in the collection: her vanity set, her hair ornaments, her love letters. My sister dissolved into tears one evening when we had finished for the day. "I feel as if I am throwing Mom and Daddy away."

But, the reality is that we couldn't keep it all. So, painstakingly, emotionally, and exasperatedly, we combed through the house as if it were an archeological dig. And, in a way, I suppose, it was.

Among the things I found was a dirty metal file box with little plastic drawers for sorting diodes, resistors, and transistors, and other early electronic parts. The box had stood on my father's workbench for as long as I can remember. At the top was my name, printed out in the same style as the labels on each drawer.

I remember the day my name came to be on that box. I was about three, and my father had received a new gadget in the mail, a label maker that used long flat spools of plastic to impress letters on. It was an exciting thing, the latest technology. I remember my father showing me what it did by painstakingly printing out the letters of my name, and then pasting the result at the top of the box.

Seeing that box on his workbench, years after his death, brought me fully back to that moment. I remembered the smell of cut metal and wood, the difficulty of seeing the top of the bench unless I were given a little stool to stand on. I remember my pride in seeing my name on the top of that box and, mostly, I remember being loved as clearly as if I had been embraced.

There is a, by now, somewhat aging trend in the world of home interiors known as "tidying up." The process, which is a method of decluttering and living a minimalist life, has an almost spiritual quality in that it claims it will change your life, and its adherents have the tone and enthusiasms of Nineteenth Century evangelists.

There is a vaguely moralistic and superior tone taken by these doyens of home organization. They are the new Puritans. No one needs stuff. No one needs other people's stuff. It is clutter. It clutters your home and your life. In this age of materialism, when we all have bulging closets, attics, basements, and enough stuff to create another entirely separate household, people's interest in the process is perfectly understandable.

But, had my father not kept his old things—radio parts that were no longer needed by any working radio—my memory of the label-making would have been lost to me, for there would have been no material thing in the world to remind me of it. That moment would have been lost to me forever.

This is the value of things, perhaps, even, of clutter. It is memories that make us who we are, that haunt us, that enrich and warm us, that remind us of how to be better. And the things, they are the memory triggers. They bring back the moments we might have forgotten in the depths of time. Memories of my mother in her kitchen or cutting off a button thread with her teeth; of my grandmother combing her hair or of picking her up at the bus station and sitting next to her in the car, touching the softness of her fur coat; of my father listening to opera at high volume while he worked on his car. These are moments that form us, that make us ourselves.

I will admit that I have kept too many things. We jokingly refer to our garage as "the home for wayward chairs." I have much of my parents' good mahogany furniture, their wing chairs, and their china cupboard. I have my grandmother's vanity. I have all my father's designs and the paperwork for his one-hundred-twenty-something patents. It is a lot, and it can be overwhelming sometimes.

But I'll take clutter any day. It is the price of remembering how it felt to be a little girl who was loved by her father.

Tidying up, indeed.

77

THE ISLAND BY NIGHT

When I am on the Island, every night, before bed, the dogs and I go out for a long walk in the dark.

There is nowhere else on earth where I could walk alone, in the dark, in the woods, and feel so completely safe. It's true, I have my dogs with me, but they are even less worried than I, and frequently slip away into the trees to leave me to the sound of my own footsteps. On a cloudy night like this, it is so dark that only the melted dirt paths of this January thaw distinguish where to walk from the white snow everywhere.

Moses, who still carries the echoes of lupine ancestors in his soul, likes to disappear into the woods, projecting my course, to silently stalk me, later to charge out onto the path in front of me in an unnerving fashion. It is a delightful game for him. Auggie, his apprentice, has begun to follow him deep among the cedar trees.

Their stealth is remarkable, and their ability to judge the intersection of vectors is proof that dogs understand geometry. Each has a red light-up collar: Moses with a slow blink and Auggie with a fast one, so when they walk with me I can tell who is who. But, when they dissolve into the woods and turn dead-on, their collars are no longer visible, and I cannot hear the sound of their padded feet, their bodies long and low, in stalking mode, until they are immediately in front of me, delighted by their prowess and by my praise. Their happiness shifts them from predators to pets, but there is an inner reality that is vital to remember.

These night walks are essential to their well-being and to mine. For them, it is a chance to reassess the activities of the local wildlife. The fox has been out since we walked this afternoon, and the raccoon and deer and possum. The turkeys are roosting in a tree somewhere near, and the deer are no doubt close by, too, waiting for the dogs to go in before they come to feed. Their game with me exhilarates the dogs and empowers them.

For me, it is an expansive moment of the soul. Alone, in the dark, but utterly unafraid, I walk along almost invisible paths, listening to the lake, to the occasional cries of owls or foxes, and I feel that I am in my life.

Nowhere else on earth.

ABOUT THE AUTHOR

Patrick Manning Photography

J. F. Riordan has worked in opera, in the classroom, and in philanthropy, but her first love is writing. Called a "modern-day Jane Austen," J.F. Riordan's lyrical prose and rich characters are a tribute to small town life, and the beauty of the ordinary. She is the author of the award winning North of the Tension Line series. Reflections on a Life in Exile is her first book of essays. She lives in Wisconsin with her husband and three big dogs.